AMONG SILENT ECHOES

Caitlin Press Inc.
3375 Ponderosa Way
Qualicum Beach, BC
V9K 2J8
www.caitlin-press.com

Text and cover design by Vici Johnstone
Edited by Betty Keller
Cover image of Carolyn as a child on her grandparents' farm in Manitoba, courtesy of the author
Printed in Canada

Caitlin Press Inc. acknowledges financial support from the Government of Canada and the Canada Council for the Arts, and the Province of British Columbia through the British Columbia Arts Council and the Book Publisher's Tax Credit.

Library and Archives Canada Cataloguing in Publication

Among silent echoes : a memoir of trauma and resilience / Phyllis Dyson.
Dyson, Phyllis, author.

Canadiana 20210200545 | ISBN 9781773860640 (softcover)

LCSH: Dyson, Phyllis—Childhood and youth. | LCSH: Dyson, Phyllis—Family. | LCSH: Adult child abuse victims—Canada—Biography. | LCSH: Adult children of dysfunctional families—Canada—Biography. | LCSH: Children of mentally ill mothers—Canada—Biography. | LCSH: Psychic trauma. | LCSH: Resilience (Personality trait) | LCGFT: Autobiographies. Classification: LCC HV6626.54.C3 D97 2021 | DDC 362.76092—dc23

AMONG SILENT ECHOES

A MEMOIR OF TRAUMA AND RESILIENCE

PHYLLIS DYSON

CAITLIN PRESS 2021

Author's Note

To write this book, I obtained newspaper articles, public records and documents through the Freedom of Information and Protection of Privacy Act. I also referred to personal journals and letters and consulted with several people who appear in the book. In some cases, to preserve anonymity, I changed names and places.

For Ron, in memory of our mother.

The Secret

I am a mystery, really so simple yet complex.
I can twist, turn and morph into many shapes and sizes.
I can be as large as a mountain or as insignificant as a flea.
I can't be touched, yet when revealed may be felt in the deepest part of one's soul.
I have the power to crumble rock or wilt a blossoming flower.
I can create ecstasy or destroy everything, even with the best intentions.
I hide behind the masks many wear, sometimes unwillingly.
There may even be wonder as to why I hide at all.
But then I wouldn't exist.

—P. Dyson

CONTENTS

Preface

There is an alarming lack of awareness surrounding mental health disorders. When my mother tragically lost her life in 1990, I didn't understand what had happened. I didn't know she was profoundly ill. It took me years to piece together the puzzle of her illness. While I was growing up in the seventies and eighties, all I heard about her formal diagnosis of paranoid schizophrenia were snippets of conversation I didn't have the knowledge to process. Any questions I had back then were either ignored or unanswered. Unfortunately silence around mental illness is common. Stigma follows mental illness like a black cloud, preventing people from talking about their symptoms and seeking help. If they are able to access help and recover, people often don't talk about their diagnosis, which prevents others from knowing how to help them if they relapse. It wasn't until I was about to become a mother myself that I gradually learned about my mother's diagnosis, first through the BC Schizophrenia Society (BCSS), then through her medical documents. I believe others will benefit from what I have learned.

Like other organs in the body, the brain can become ill. Mental illnesses are common and treatable medical disorders caused by a complex interplay of genetic, biological, personality and environmental factors. They usually emerge between the ages of fifteen and twenty-four, but they affect people of all ages and do not differentiate by economic status or culture.

People with schizophrenia are highly vulnerable. Cognitive deficits such as limited attention, memory loss, problem-solving difficulties and poor coping skills are prevalent and can limit a person's quality of life, which can lead to depression, a risk factor for suicide. People with schizophrenia experience a higher risk for suicide than with any other illness.

Cognitive deficits can affect a person's access to quality employment. Unable to earn a livable wage, the person may struggle to survive, causing anxiety levels to rise, which can trigger a relapse. Since psychiatric care has largely moved from hospital-based to community-based care, greatly reducing the number of beds, patients are often released before they are stabilized. Many are caught in a revolving-door pattern of care. With each successive relapse, the brain takes longer to heal. Some individuals may never recover and become homeless wanderers of the streets.

Owing to a lack of supportive and affordable housing, some individuals live with a family member who often becomes their primary caregiver. If there happens to be lack of awareness, as there often is with mental illness, blame and shame can lie beneath the surface and tensions can rise, further contributing to the risk of a relapse.

Those who experience psychotic symptoms such as hallucinations (hearing voices) or paranoia may either become victims of scorn or not be taken seriously even while in recovery. This can lead to feelings of guilt and shame, which can trigger people to go off their antipsychotic medication or even attempt suicide. Others may turn to marijuana, which can exacerbate symptoms, or to street drugs, which can cause a concurrent disorder of addiction.

Though hallucinations and delusions are not real, they appear real to the person experiencing them and can be frightening. Voices may tell individuals to hurt themselves or make them believe others are going to hurt them. When people become this acutely ill, psychiatric hospital care is essential and can be complicated because they may not recognize they are ill (a condition called anosognosia) and may resist help. A person in psychosis is often scared and may become aggressive. To ensure safety and preserve as much dignity as possible, a first responder with mental health training, equipped with the skills to calmly de-escalate a situation, is optimal. Sadly this is often not the case and tragedy can ensue. At times, psychotic illness is even criminalized.

There is hope. With a combination of counselling, education, medication, housing and hospital- and community-based care, long-term recovery is possible. Non-profit organizations like the BCSS advocate for those who experience serious mental illness, offering educational programs for all ages that increase awareness and encourage people to talk about their experiences so they know they are not alone.

I have talked to my daughters about mental illness. They are keenly aware of the genetic factors contributing to their risk of developing the same biological disorder as my mother. They know that heavy drinking could cause the loss of precious brain cells they need for optimal functioning and have learned that marijuana and other street drugs could trigger psychosis and exacerbate symptoms.

Another positive is BC's formation of the Ministry of Mental Health and Addictions, a first in Canada. BC's *A Pathway to Hope* plan describes "a powerful determination to make positive, lasting changes, so that BC's system of mental health and addictions care works for everyone—no matter who they are, where they live, or how much money they make."[1] I only hope my story will help facilitate these changes by breaking silences and increasing compassion for those affected by serious mental illness.

1   Province of British Columbia, *A Pathway to Hope: A Roadmap for Making Mental Health and Addictions Care Better for People in British Columbia*, 3, https://www2.gov. bc.ca/assets/gov/british-columbians-our-governments/initiatives-plans-strategies/ mental-health-and-addictions-strategy/bcmentalhealthroadmap_2019web-5.pdf.

Part One

INTRODUCTION

April 2015
I rarely talk about my parents. I was estranged from my father when I was very young, so I don't have much to say about him. My mother died the summer of 1990 when I was in college, and the burden of her death is so shameful that I don't know *what* to say about her. If anyone asks, I'm always careful not to reveal too much about her, determined to keep my secret.

I did the same when my younger daughter rattled me with her questions one evening. It was her bedtime and I had just closed her curtains to shade the room from the light of the long spring days. My husband was tinkering in his workshop as he often does in the evenings, and my older daughter was reading in the living room. As I sat beside my daughter while she lay under her comforter, I gazed into her golden-green eyes, admiring her strawberry hair splayed across her pillow and the splash of freckles across her nose.

"Mummy?" she asked.

"Yes, love?"

"How old was your mom when she died?"

What? Where did this come from? "She was forty-five," I answered, keeping emotion out of my voice, not giving anything away. She was silent for a few moments and looked deep in thought.

"How old were you?"

"I was twenty." *Only ten years older than you are now.*

"That's really sad, Mum."

"Yes, I know. It's very sad, but it was a long time ago. My mother was sick, but I'm healthy. I'm fine," I said, assuring her in case she was making the connection that I was now forty-five myself. "Come now, you have school tomorrow," I said, changing the subject as I often did at the mention of my mother. After singing our special bedtime song, I hugged her tightly, bid her good night and then walked to my room to sit down. Her questions had thrown me off-kilter and I needed to collect myself. I've never told my daughters the details surrounding my mother's death. That wouldn't be appropriate. I had told them that my mother died of "complications" due to schizophrenia. Now, my daughter's curiosity made me wonder if one day she would want to know how her grandmother had *really* died and how I would reveal the secret burden I have carried all these years.

WOMAN KILLED

Plain-Clothes RCMP Fires Two Shots
New Westminster Now, vol. 2, no. 29, July 29, 1990

The police officer who shot and killed a New West-minster woman at a downtown SkyTrain station is a member of the Vancouver RCMP who was working on cleaning up the downtown area at the time of the shooting.

The unidentified plain-clothes officer is a member of a special joint-forces squad of the New Westminster police department and the RCMP, according to a NWPD police spokesperson.

During recent weeks police had been cracking down on illegal activities in the downtown area. ...

The shooting occurred at 8 p.m. on Tuesday night when quite a few late commuters were in the station. According to police the NWPD received several calls about a woman shouting and threatening passersby with a large knife on the concourse level of the 8th St. Sky-Train station. Some witnesses later said the knife looked like a butcher's variety.

According to the police, the RCMP officer was the first to arrive at the scene. He then identified himself as a police officer and removed his service revolver from its holster. The officer then ordered the woman to drop the knife. According [to] the police the woman ignored the officer's orders and continued to approach him with the knife. Police say she was running towards the officer.

As the police officer backed away from the woman he stumbled and fell to the ground on his back. The woman then allegedly continued to approach the offi-cer until she reached his feet and then she pointed the knife at him.

When the woman stood over the officer with the knife raised, the officer, fearing for his life, fired two rounds from his service revolver, police said. A witness at the scene said it looked like she had been shot in the stomach and chest.

Carolyn Anne ... , 45, died shortly after being rushed to Royal Columbian Hospital. The police officer did not receive any injuries. ...

THE REVELATION

It was June 2015, and my mind was spinning. I had just spent an afternoon learning about psychotic disorders. Now, seeing my mother through a lens of understanding I'd never had before, I felt as if she had died not years ago but yesterday. As I steered my sedan homeward along a winding rural road, three words kept echoing in my head like a scratched record skipping: *stress, relapse, recovery … stress, relapse, recovery …*

Home in my quiet neighbourhood minutes later, I opened my front door and called out a greeting. After hearing replies from the rec room where my family was watching television, I walked upstairs to take a shower, partly because I was sticky from the summer heat but mostly because I didn't want my family to hear the release of emotions for the loss of my mother I'd somehow managed to keep inside me all afternoon: tears of compassion for an illness she never asked for, tears of sadness for her short, misunderstood life and tears of frustration for the time together we could have had if it hadn't been brutally taken away.

My mother had needed help, not bullets.

Years ago, as a naive college kid, I had found the blow of her death too surreal, too overwhelming to process. I remember there was a reporter who kept showing up at the apartment complex where I shared a rental with my brother, who always happened to be at his day job when the guy came. I didn't want to talk to a reporter. *Leave me alone.* One evening as my boyfriend, John, and I were about to head out for a quiet dinner, the phone rang the special buzzer tone that told me someone wanted into the building. *Bzzzz, bzzzz.*

"Oh, great, I think it's that reporter again," I said. "I'm not expecting anybody."

"I'll go down and check." When he came back, he confirmed, "Yep, it's a reporter."

"What should we do?"

"Let's just wait a few minutes. He'll probably be gone by then."

While we sat quietly on my second-hand couch, his arm wrapped around me, my eyes prickled with tears. I gazed around the apartment. On the counter I saw the dish rack Mom had brought me only a few months earlier, the one she had found in her apartment building's dumpster and cleaned up good as new.

"When I was by, I noticed you didn't have one," she'd said. "There's nothing wrong with this one. It's fine. Somebody was throwing it out." She couldn't help me a lot, as she was getting by on disability, but she did what she could.

When John went downstairs again a few minutes later, the reporter was gone, so we left.

—∞—

Somehow I had kept looking forward after that, almost as if I'd never had a mother. It was the same for my brother, Ron, eighteen months older than me. Throughout our childhood, whenever the road had unexpectedly veered down a sketchy path, with our mother nearly losing us completely along the way, we'd held each other up, navigating the unexpected turns together. It had been too hard to look back. Now, after my daughter's question, all my mind wanted to do was look back.

Over the days that followed, as a busy teacher and mother, I managed to keep my thoughts in the present. But at night, when everything was quiet, I lay awake for hours, thinking of the past, thinking about my mother, who I know did the best she could. "We were her everything," Ron had once said.

Our mother was usually calm, gentle and shy, especially in public. She pretty much kept to herself, a person in a crowd quietly running errands, not getting in anyone's way, barely noticeable. She would give my brother or me her last few dollars if she thought we needed it more. She never asked us for anything and never complained to us about being poor. She smelled of Ivory soap, cigarette smoke, waxy lipstick and cheap perfume. She enjoyed a good joke and *The Price Is Right*. Her idea of a good time was listening to records, swimming at the lake or tossing a Frisbee at the park.

The media took notice of her once she was dead. I remember sitting in John's pickup the day after she died, heading to the beach in an attempt to escape the shock of it all. We were listening to Tom Petty's big summer hit "Free Fallin'.""When the song ended, there was a news flash. "A woman was shot in the Lower Mainland yesterday. There could be a connection to drug trafficking." I reached over and switched off the radio.

A few days later Mom was turned into a headline. I remember Ron and me reading about her in disbelief. We knew she had schizophrenia and that she occasionally expressed a negative attitude toward men, but we don't remember her ever acting the way she was described in the paper. And we'd certainly *never* seen her run at anyone. The only person we'd ever heard she'd gone after with a knife was our father, a sheet metal worker she'd met at a bus stop back in Ottawa where the family lived at the time, having moved from small-town Manitoba where my mother was born. He'd asked her for a smoke, and they'd married a couple of years later. Her parents and younger siblings—her sister, Lynn, and two brothers, Walter and Jack—could hardly believe she'd married at all.

A couple of years later, with Mom trying to balance parenthood with schizophrenia and our father returning to their downtown rental drunk in the early morning hours, wedded bliss had evaporated. Family lore has it that when Ron was a toddler and I was an infant, our parents had a heated argument. Mom had grabbed a knife, missed her target and cut me instead. She hadn't meant to. I know she would never have hurt me on purpose. I have no recollection of the incident, but there's a scar on my left shin, paler than the rest of my skin and just over an inch long.

By then my grandparents had settled with their teenaged sons on the West Coast, where my grandfather's government job had been transferred, leaving their married daughters in the country's booming capital. It wasn't long before my grandmother flew halfway across the country to rescue us. Ron was two and a half and I was barely one when, under the cover of daylight while my father was wielding a work hammer, my grandmother helped my mother sling diapers and clothes into a suitcase, then they tucked Ron and me under their arms and headed to the airport. I wonder now what our father thought when he came home to find us gone. We didn't hear from him for many years.

My grandmother took us to Burnaby, British Columbia, where the memory of my life begins and where secrets lay waiting to be unearthed.

Part Two

THE CASTLE

My earliest memory is of a brick castle perched atop a grassy hill. I was three years old. It must have been early in the fall of 1972. The grass was still lusciously green and the air comfortably warm. In a few moments I would realize that it was not a castle at all, but for now I was full of awe as I sat in the back seat of my grandmother's sleek, black 1964 Chrysler, my brother beside me. She turned the corner then and drove up a long, winding driveway to park behind the vast building. My thoughts were filled with wonder as Ron and I got out of the car.

"Come, Ronnie! Come, Phyllis. It's this way," my grandmother said, taking our hands.

We walked up wide concrete steps as I took in the sight of the building, but the moment we entered through its doors, all thoughts of castles floated away. I saw flashes of light, a shiny grey floor and tall windows with beams of sunlight shining into a dull room as nurses strutted like seagulls on a sandy beach. I was in a hospital waiting to see my mother. I have tried to capture her face and what she was wearing, for I know she was the reason I was there, but my only other memory of that day is playing on the lush green lawn with my brother, running and laughing among large deciduous trees. The rest is gone, lost with the ticking of time.

I have other memories of those early days, cheerful ones of mild afternoons at the park. Mom and her boyfriend, Gilbert, a construction worker whom I now believe she met in the hospital, would push Ron and me on the swings in the courtyard of our low-income East Hastings Street complex. After Mom pushed us up to the pale blue sky, Gilbert would give us "underducks" and we'd gleefully shout, "Again! Again! Higher, higher!"

Other afternoons the air would be full of excitement as we travelled down Canada Way in Gilbert's hatchback to Moody Park for an alfresco lunch. After sandwiches and potato salad, Ron and I were happy to dig in the sandbox with plastic shovels while Mom and Gilbert lay on a blanket enjoying each other's company. Mom would be smiling, looking young and pretty in her crop pants and blouse, the raven-black hair that she brushed a hundred strokes every night styled in a 1960s flip. I remember falling asleep many nights in the bed we shared, the momentum of her movements lulling me to sleep as she sat at the vanity brushing her beautiful locks.

But I also have memories of fear. One afternoon the front passenger door of Gilbert's hatchback suddenly vanished as the two of us were heading down Hastings to run errands. I was looking out the front window at the passing buildings when I heard a sudden increase in traffic noise and felt wind rush onto my body. I was startled when I looked beside me to see that the door was gone. Instead, there was a blur of pavement inches away from my Mary Janed feet. When I raised my eyes, I saw the look of alarm in the eyes of another driver as he passed. I dared not move. That was when I noticed the door was there again, swinging almost closed, then wide open again. Back and forth it went, swinging on its hinges. I was too young to have the strength, let alone the courage, to reach out and pull it shut. All I could do was sit still and not move a muscle. Gilbert looked over then and must have seen the fright in my eyes. "Holy shit!" he said. We were driving past a mini-mall, and moments later, while stopped at an intersection, he was finally able to lean over me and shut the door that he'd entrusted my three-year-old muscles to manage before we'd headed off.

Then there was my fear of loud explosions of shouting, the sudden changes from peace to war. Ron and I would be playing in the front room when the volume in the apartment would rise with the noise of my mother screeching and Gilbert yelling, angry words flying across the room. I'd sit motionless in silent alarm, not knowing what to do.

"You don't love me anymore!" Mom yelled one day.

"Yes, I do," Gilbert assured her.

"Why don't you ever answer the phone when I call? You're lying!"

"I told you, my phone's disconnected because I'm moving in here soon!"

"I don't believe you! You're just like all the other dirty rotten men in the world. All cheats and liars!"

"Oh my God, Carolyn! Why don't you ever listen? There's no reasoning with you! Why do I even bother?" Gilbert yelled back.

Just as quickly as the war began, peace would return with the loud slam of Gilbert walking out the door, and Mom would lie alone in her bedroom, leaving Ron and me to our toys. A day or so later Gilbert would return. Everything would go back to happy families again, but it was too good to last. Before long, the arguments would start again. More angry words, more slamming doors. One day Gilbert walked out the door without even saying goodbye.

Mom must have been heartbroken, not to mention lonely, when he left. I think Gilbert had been her only friend. She'd told her doctor, the same doctor who'd described her as "quite crazy," that she couldn't make friends on the "outside." Now she didn't even take us to the daycare we'd attended on occasion. She'd sleep for hours instead. When I'd wake beside her and nudge her to get up, all she would do was groan.

Ron and I learned to fend for ourselves. We'd pour our own cereal and milk, then dump the toy box in the living room, and in the light coming from the sliding balcony doors, he would push his plastic trucks while I'd set up tea parties and picnics for my dolls. Eventually Mom would come out of the bedroom into the light, though the first thing she would do was ignite a smoke and drag herself to the couch to stare at us with a tired, blank gaze without a hint of a smile.

One morning Ron decided we should play drums to wake her up. I was too young to understand his plan but happy to help out. We pulled every pot and pan we could find out of the cupboards, placed them upside down on the kitchen floor, then belted out the alphabet song as we banged on our steel drums with the wooden spoons we'd found in a drawer. "A, B, C, D, E, F, G!"

His plan worked. I was having a glorious time following his lead when Mom appeared wearing her baby-blue robe, her thick black hair dishevelled, to spoil our singing fun. "Stop that racket!" she yelled.

That was the only time we tried that, but Ron had another plan. With Mom too tired to move and my brother too tired of her not moving, one day he left me to entertain myself while he walked to our grandparents' house. We had stayed with them for some time when we'd first moved west, until, as documented in my mother's medical files, "her father couldn't cope with her moods because he found them too upsetting." They lived about twenty blocks away, and as Ron walked, people driving by would notice this little boy walking alone on the sidewalk. Some would roll down their windows and offer him a ride. He always turned them down. Later he'd get a scolding. "You're too young to walk all that way by yourself," Mom and Granny would say, but he had kept on walking until one day a police officer picked him up.

After that, Granny, a petite lady like my mother, came around more often. After we jumped around her in excitement, she'd unpack the groceries she'd brought and then talk to Mom in the bedroom. I'd hear their low, muttering voices while I played. At times she'd come into the front room looking as tired as Mom, letting out a sigh. To cheer her up, I'd climb onto her lap and sing "Patty Cake." Ron would take turns in the fun too, and before long Granny was all smiles again. But one morning she and Mom exchanged louder words than usual.

"You can't have them! They're *my* children!" Mom yelled. While I didn't understand what was happening then, I see now that my grandmother had grown totally frustrated with my deeply depressed mother. Moments later Mom somehow mustered the energy to get up. Silently we watched her wander into the room in her dark-rimmed glasses, a baggy blouse and her signature polyester slacks, her hair loose rather than prettily styled. She settled on the couch and lit a cigarette, her zombie face hidden behind clouds of smoke. Granny, meanwhile, lightened the mood by performing somersaults and headstands on the shag carpet, encouraging Ron and me to copy her.

As the days passed with the three of us rolling around, Mom eventually came back to life, playfully shouting, "Watch the coffee table! Look out for the couch!"

⟶

By the time I was four, Mom was getting up in time to get Ron off to school. After a cold breakfast, we'd walk him to morning kindergarten and then usually take the bus down Hastings Street. She kept a transit schedule in her purse, a white and blue brochure that folded up like a road map. Hastings was all hustle and bustle with stores, restaurants and produce stands, and Mom would walk quickly in and out of stores, holding my hand.

"Come on, Phyllis. We don't have time to dawdle. We have to get Ronnie from school soon," she'd say, tugging my arm to encourage me to keep up.

She'd be focused on her errands, but I was more interested in looking in the shop windows, especially the displays of elaborate dresses in the bridal stores. I'd imagine myself wearing one with puffed sleeves and twirling like a princess. If I wasn't admiring the dresses, I would stand outside a children's clothing store, mesmerized by the momentum of the neon sign overhead of a girl on a swing, a girl with brunette hair, blue shoes and a pink skirt. I couldn't read then, but when I was older I learned the store's name was Helen's.

One day Mom took me inside, and my heart raced as I willed her to buy me a pretty dress. It seems odd to me now that instead of walking with her, I stood by the door observing her as she moved around the shop, her face like stone. She seemed so distant at times, as if she wasn't there even though she was in the same room. I know now that a lack of facial expression can be a symptom of schizophrenia, but as a four-year-old, I just stood quietly near the entrance tracking her movements while she calmly walked around in her slow gait, pausing here and there to glance at the price tag on a pair of children's slacks or a practical-looking top, not giving away any emotion, before she walked back out and I fell into step behind her. She hadn't even glanced at dresses.

Not that I didn't have any. I know I had a green velvet holiday dress. Back then, we celebrated Christmas with my grandparents, and Granddad always sent Ron and me into giggling fits with his whisker-rub greetings. It was a family tradition to take pictures in front of the tree in those days, and in one of those photos, Mom and I are wearing matching green dresses while Ron, grinning widely, is dressed in plaid pants, a white, long-sleeved shirt and a beige woollen vest. We are kneeling among our new treasures: a Raggedy Ann doll, a wooden train, a Pinocchio record and a huge stuffed reindeer, Rudolph, that was almost as big as I was with its antlers, long legs and, of course, its red nose.

I'm pretty sure that Uncle Jack must have shown up at my grandparents' house on those occasions too. He wouldn't miss a home-cooked meal. He was a fun-loving guy with dark hair and glasses like my mother's. Ron and I would have eagerly shown him our gifts, then giggled as he crawled around on all fours to give us horse rides while Mom and Granny prepared the festive meal and Granddad worked in his den until the table was generously laid with platters of turkey, ham and vegetables. There was always a good spread at my grandparents' house.

It wouldn't have been too many weeks afterwards, while Ron was in school, that Mom and I got off the bus at a medical office, which wasn't the usual office we went to. The usual place was on the side of a hill in a brown and white building that was so tall it looked as though it would fall over. We had to climb up a dimly lit stairwell of what seemed like a hundred stairs to the top floor. Mom would take us there to see our doctor, a tall man with dark hair, if we had the flu or a cold.

This time we were in a building near Brentwood Mall, and it wasn't a doctor but a nurse who greeted us. As we walked into a small room with a desk, a couple of chairs and small, high windows, she directed me to have a seat. I watched curiously as she prepared a needle with Mom standing opposite her. Then Mom bent over and pulled down her pants, in and out went the needle, up went the pants and the appointment was over. At the time I had no idea what had just happened. I know now that my mother had just received her medication by injection.

Smoke and Fire

"Wow! This house is so big!" Ron and I exclaimed as we ran around our new home, excited that it was so much roomier than our apartment. "Look at the backyard!" we yelled as we bolted from our empty bedrooms down the stairs to the door.

"Slow down! No running inside!" Mom yelled as she and Uncle Jack wrestled with boxes and furniture.

We had moved into the top two floors of a three-storey 1940s wood-framed house with stucco siding on Royal Oak Avenue in Burnaby, next to an industrial area of warehouses. Mom and I shared a room on the top floor down the hall from Ron's room, while Uncle Jack, who would share the rent because, I realize now, Mom couldn't afford the place otherwise, had a room on the floor below, just off the living room. It wasn't long before Mom had the place warm and welcoming, as if we'd been living there for years, with the furniture neatly arranged and the window ledges decorated with the miniature porcelain figures we found in boxes of Red Rose tea. "Look, it's a kitten this time! Aww." Over the next weeks Ron and I would forage for blackberries in the backyard until our fingers turned purple. We also took swimming lessons at the nearby rec centre, and I remember Ron kicking up a fuss because he wasn't thrilled with having to dress in the women's change room with his mother and little sister.

Looking back at that time, with Mom in a period of recovery, I think we were happy for the most part. She made a new friend of the lady who lived next door. Betty was older than my mother and had salt and pepper hair, but like my mother, she enjoyed her cigarettes. "Carolyn, why don'cha come over fo' coffee?" she'd yell from her back porch with a smoke dangling from her mouth. It was a miracle the cigarette didn't fall out. Mom would rise from her chair on the porch and saunter over with her pack of Player's Light. They'd sit for hours in Betty's kitchen, chatting and laughing, while Ron and I hunted for bugs or played tag in the yard with Betty's daughter, Lorraine, who was a few years older than Ron. She had kind blue eyes and a ready smile, and we both adored her. I think now that she was Ron's first crush.

A gentle old man with a wrinkled, leathery face, likely an old-age pensioner, lived downstairs. He'd often sit in his dressing gown on a rickety chair on the lower back landing, puffing on a cigarette and watching us kids playing. He was the one who gave Ron, aged six, his first opportunity in money management. I remember him calling my brother over and filling his hands with coins to fetch milk or bread for him from the corner store across the street. He let my brother keep the change, which he squirrelled away. I think I was too young to understand the responsibility involved because I don't remember being upset that I wasn't asked to go. I do remember Ron being kind enough to share some of the red licorice he bought and feeding some of it to our pet hamster. While we were enjoying the chewy sweetness, I had asked, "Do you think Snuffles likes candy?"

"I don't know," he'd answered. "Let's find out."

We put some pieces through the bars of the cage and within moments we were thrilled when Snuffles ate the little bits. "He likes it!" But after Snuffles coughed up red mush, we quickly retreated before Mom could see us. When she cleaned the cage a day or so later, we just looked at each other when she yelled, "What have you been feeding him?" Only weeks later, when we gave our pet a break from being enclosed in its cage, Snuffles made a run for freedom, escaping out an open window and leaving us crestfallen.

While Ron was learning to manage money, I was learning to make cigarettes, and by age five I could make a perfect rollie. On the porch one evening I'd watched Mom make them with her cigarette maker and, mesmerized by the process, asked if I could try. "Sure!" Eagerly I tucked a Zig-Zag paper into the mini conveyor belt, added a large pinch of coarse tobacco from Mom's Player's tin, making sure to spread it out evenly, then slid the mechanism, which operated like a manual credit card machine. Swish! I was disappointed when the first cigarette I'd fashioned was like an overstuffed wrap, the paper not sealed and tobacco bursting out, but Mom patiently encouraged me to try again. "You used too much tobacco." I gave it another shot, adding a twist at the end. Presto! I had made a perfect rollie! I continued to make many more, proudly storing each one of them in the flat, tarnished silver tin Mom kept in her purse.

Ron and I had fun playing games with Uncle Jack, giggling hysterically at his horse bites and whisker rubs, running around, feigning fear. "No, Uncle Jack, no! Not a horse bite," my brother and I would yell, laughing as he tried to pinch our upper thighs as we scrambled away.

Mom would often join in the fun too. "Run, run! He's coming for you!"

"I'm going to get you! Here I come!" he'd yell. If we were caught, we'd be in for it. He loved to make silly faces too. At mealtimes, he'd pull his glasses halfway down his face, cross his eyes and stick out his tongue. Other times, he'd pull out his trombone and have us frolicking around the room to tunes like "When the Saints Go Marching In" and "Auld Lang Syne."

In September when school started, Mom walked us there each morning. I'd usually chatter about the games I played with my classmates at recess and lunch, but whenever I told her I was looking forward to playing boys chase the girls, she'd say, "You be careful with those boys. They're only after one thing, you know." Eventually I stopped telling her about the fun of the chase, tired of her repeated warnings, though not fully understanding her words. Usually, through puffs of smoke, she would talk about her plans for the day. She liked routine. Every day she'd do a different job, like the laundry, dusting or dishes. "When I get home, I'll have a coffee break. Then I think I'll dust the living room." Looking back, I have realized that routine probably helped her cope with cognitive deficits like memory loss and poor organizational skills as a result of having schizophrenia, which likely also affected her vocational abilities and social skills.

Unfortunately it wasn't all fun and games at our house. Like all the adults around us who smoked, perhaps to pass the idle time or release nervous energy, Uncle Jack liked his cigarettes, so much so that he'd light up in bed. I'd often wake in the middle of the night to Mom pounding on his bedroom door. *Bang! Bang! Bang!* "Jack! Put out that cigarette! I can tell you're smoking in there. Put that out right now! You better not fall asleep smoking or I'll crown you! Do you hear me?"

"Shut up! Leave me alone. I can do what I want!" he'd shout back.

And on they'd go. I learned to ignore the noise, roll over and fall back to sleep. In the mornings, as we ate the hot Sunny Boy Cereal Mom had prepared, she'd often say, "Jack's going to burn this place down if he keeps smoking in bed. I wish he'd listen to me," and she'd shake her head.

They argued about meals too. Jack wasn't courteous enough to let Mom know his plans. "How am I supposed to know how much food to cook?" she said angrily when he walked through the front door one evening. "How can I make any plans when half the time you're not here?"

"I got my own stuff to do!"

"'Own stuff to do'? You don't even have a job! What do you do all day? No wonder you don't have a girlfriend. When you're here, you just sleep the day away. You're just a lazy good-for-nothin'!" Then Jack would go to his room and slam the door.

The stress of their arguments would set Mom off, ranting about men. "Don't ever get married, Phyllis. Men are pigs!" she'd say. Not knowing how to respond, I wouldn't react. To avoid their nightly arguments, Ron and I would play outdoors, which was easy to do with summer's clear days and long evenings. Other times we'd retire to our rooms in an attempt to escape the noise.

It was easy to forget about this unpleasantness when Mom took us on outings. We always took the city bus. She would usually stare straight ahead while Ron and I looked out the window. I'd pass the time rating houses in my head on a scale of one to ten, imagining the kind of house I wanted. I had certain criteria: the house had to be tidy looking, not too big but with lots of windows, and have a nice flower garden and a large, well-tended grassy yard. But I had to be quick with my rating as the bus moved fast. *Eight—that house is nice, not too big, nice tidy yard and it has a balcony too ... oh, not that one, it doesn't have a garden and it's messy looking, needs a paint job, it's just a five ...* I rated houses this way for years.

When our stop was near, both Ron and I liked to pull the cord, which caused the occasional argument. "Are we there yet? Should I pull it?" Ron would say.

"It's my turn!" I'd pipe up, wanting to be first.

"No, it's mine!"

"You pulled it last time!"

"Enough!" Mom would intervene, pulling the cord. Ron and I would shoot angry looks at each other, but we'd quickly forget about our petty disagreement once we arrived at our destination.

—✦—

A favourite place was Deer Lake, a quiet piece of beauty off Sperling Avenue in Burnaby. I remember those scorching hot days and Ron and me running down the sidewalk in the shade of the park trees, a bag of towels in hand.

"Step on a crack, break your mother's back!" he would yell.

"Come on, Mom!" I'd turn and shout. "Hurry up!" Eager to cool off, I jumped across the cracks, getting into a rhythm.

"I'm coming. We'll get there," she'd reply in a playful voice, smoking while she continued to walk at her calm, steady pace. "Make sure I can see you, and watch for cars!" she'd yell.

Ron and I would always get there first, and it took all the patience we had to wait for her. When she'd finally arrive, we'd carefully choose a place to camp for the day and lay down the blanket she'd brought on a spot that was clear of goose droppings. (The combination of water and grass was a great attraction for Canada geese.) As we wore our bathing suits underneath, Ron and I would whip off our clothes and run into the lake. "Race you!" he'd yell. He always beat me, but I didn't care because I was in heaven. Moments later Mom would join us in the water and start a splashing fight. There was always plenty of laughter and squeals of delight. After an hour or so we'd head for the blanket to have our packed lunch of sandwiches and apples. Water would drip on our food, turning it soggy, but we didn't care. Everything tastes better outdoors in the sunshine. Mom would teasingly call us "nitwits." Nitwits. We thought it was so funny.

There was a concession nearby, but we never bought anything. It never even occurred to Ron and me to ask. We were happy to spend the day at the beach. After lunch, while Mom relaxed on the blanket with a cigarette, we'd trail our towels down our back as capes and swoop around like the superheroes we saw on Saturday-morning cartoons. Later we'd leave her to her thoughts while we walked the trail at the lake's edge, where ducks hid in the reeds and water spiders skidded magically across the water. Afterwards Mom would push us on the swings.

One sweltering afternoon as I swung back and forth, I noticed a large building on the other side of the lake.

"What's that, Mom?" I asked, pointing.

"That's the Oakalla Prison," Mom replied.

"What's a prison?" I asked.

"It's a place where bad people go, people who break the law," she said.

I nodded and didn't think any more about it, not then.

⟋⟍

Another of our summer destinations was Stanley Park. I liked watching the landscape change from the shops and houses and lawns where we lived in Burnaby to the city's tall buildings and beyond them the mountains and sea. For this trip we had to travel downtown on a gas bus, then wait at the downtown hub for an electric trolley bus. While waiting, I would be mesmerized by the web of black cables spreading across the sky, and I can still hear the clicking as the poles passed the connections where the overhead cables met. Sometimes when the poles happened to disconnect and the bus stopped, Ron and I would run with excitement to an empty window seat to watch the driver direct them back onto their tracks, and then we'd be off on our way again.

We would disembark opposite the water fountain at Lost Lagoon, and after Mom lit her cigarette, we'd walk along the paved pathway. I remember the first time I hand fed a squirrel there. When we reached the point where the trees edged the path, I could hear him chattering.

"Look, Mom, there's a squirrel!" I shouted as it ran up a tree and remained magically clinging there.

"Mom, there's one eating out of that man's hand! Can we feed them?" asked Ron.

She stopped and pulled a sandwich from our picnic basket. "Give him just a little bit," she said. "We have to save some for our lunch."

"What about me, Mom? I want a turn!" I complained.

She handed me a sandwich morsel too, then said, "Hold your hand out straight, stay calm and don't move or you'll scare it."

"It's coming toward me! It's coming!" I said, but then suddenly it darted away.

"Be patient," Mom said, "and it'll come back."

I crouched low, barely breathing. Then out of nowhere the squirrel returned. It took all my self-control to be still and calm so as not to ruin the moment.

"I did it, Mom. I did it! Did you see? That black squirrel ate right out of my hand!" And we laughed.

"We fed the squirrels!" Ron said, encouraging me to run along the path. "Let's go!"

"Don't get too far ahead! I have to be able to see you."

"We won't, Mom! We won't!"

We spent hours admiring the various animals caged in the zoo. (This was before animal rights activists intervened on their behalf.) Cream-coloured polar bears lazing in the sun, penguins waddling along in their black and white suits, swinging and chattering monkeys with arms that seemed too long for their bodies and—my favourite animal to this day—the sleek otters teasing their admiring audience as they went up and down their slide.

"Look, Mom! That otter is taking its baby for a ride," I said as an otter swam around on its back with its young on its belly.

"Well, look at that! They certainly are cute," said Mom.

Ron especially liked looking through the windows of the reptile cells. There were snakes coiled up in the corners or hanging out of miniature trees and lizards hiding among the grass and rocks, and it was a game trying to find them as they blended so completely into their surroundings. While we ate our picnic lunch, we watched people feed the shiny green-hooded ducks, snowy-white swans and ducks with flashes of purple tucked into their wings. We never saw the orca or dolphin shows because we would have had to pay, but it was thrilling enough to hear their splashes and the cheers and clapping of the crowd. In the late afternoon we headed home with visions in our heads of playful animals that we talked about for days, and wonderful memories we would cherish for a lifetime.

———

It was my mother who sparked my love of reading. She'd take us to the Burnaby Public Library, where Ron and I would make our selections by pulling books off the shelves and reading the covers. If the titles were too hard for us to read, Mom would read them for us. I liked fairy tales or Dr. Seuss, while Ron preferred books about trucks or bugs. When it was time to leave, we'd walk proudly to the front desk, our library cards in hand. Later that evening Mom would read our selections to us. "Once upon a time in a faraway land lived ..." she'd begin, pointing to the words, while Ron and I sat on either side of her on the sofa. As my reading skills steadily improved, her tracking began to drive me crazy. I would often read ahead and her hand would get in my way, but I never complained. She was so proud of my reading skills. "You're a good reader because of me," she'd say. "I always pointed to the words for you."

A nice change from taking the bus was walking up the road to the community centre, which was a big old house that had been transformed into a place for families like ours to hang out. While I can't remember any of the staff specifically, I remember that they were a little younger than Mom, and they were always sunny and welcoming. "Hi, Carolyn!" they'd say, then cheerily chat with our mother while Ron and I were entertained by the many activities. Ron liked playing foosball or table hockey, while I preferred to read, sitting on the worn sofa in the quiet of the book room away from the clattering noise and whooping celebrations.

One weekend the staff organized a camping trip in a wooded area not too far out of the city. We slept in a tent, roasted marshmallows and sang songs by the campfire. I liked roasting marshmallows the best. I remember a staff member taking Ron and me to the edge of the forest to cut aspen branches and then sharpen them to a point with her jackknife so we could use them as roasting sticks. After watching other campers burn their marshmallows in the flames, I learned to place mine just above the glowing orange coals, turning it carefully so each section would turn amber. I was able to roast some of mine pretty close to perfection, but others ended up in flames, and the adult campers were quick to yell, "Blow it out!" By then my luscious marshmallow was a black blistery glob. Mom ate those as she didn't mind that they had turned to charcoal. She would put her marshmallow directly into the flame, burn it black, then eat it after it was cool, enjoying its gooeyness. And every time someone else's marshmallow caught fire, she would claim it. "I'll eat it if nobody else wants it!" she'd say. I don't know how she could stand it, but to each her own.

To this day one of my most vivid memories of that outing was her radiant smile the following morning. Ron and I had already risen with the dawn and were sitting on stumps by the fire, enjoying hot chocolate with the other campers. "Good morning!" she said, her smiling face beaming at us through the open tent flap. She was so happy.

—⸎⸎—

Later that year Ron and I met our mother's brother Walter, his wife and our infant cousin. It was a sunny afternoon at our grandparents' house, and shortly after arriving, Mom and Granny got busy with dinner preparations and Granddad disappeared into his den. Ron and I went outside to enjoy the warm weather, and when we wandered into the backyard, we discovered a young man with black hair and glasses like Mom's playing catch, gently throwing an air-filled ball to a toddler who teetered around as he attempted to catch it, then giggled and fell over. A young woman in jeans and a halter top was sunning on a blanket nearby.

"Hi, Phyllis. Hi, Ronnie," the young man said. "You probably don't remember me. I'm your uncle Walter. This here is Patrick. We call him Pat. And this is Stacy," he said warmly as the young woman smiled.

After eyeing them shyly, Ron went off to ride the red tricycle kept in our grandparents' garage, while I stayed to play catch with Walter and Pat, tossing the ball around and laughing. I tried to visit with Stacy, too, who I would later learn had been Walter's high school sweetheart, but she wouldn't look at me, keeping her eyes always on Pat, her pride and joy.

Later, after Granddad emerged from his office, we enjoyed a hearty feast, sitting around the dining table away from the cool evening air, with Uncle Jack showing up just in time, eager for a good meal.

—⸎⸎—

"Make sure you stop at the intersection, Phyllis, and stay away from the curb," Ron ordered as we walked down a busy section of Imperial Street one morning. At seven, he took his older-brother role seriously. Now that we were in school full-time, Mom had taken a part-time job as a keypunch operator. After a cold breakfast, she'd send us off with our bagged lunches, head for work and then be home by the time we returned. The odd time that she started work early, she trusted Uncle Jack to get us off to school, which was all right by me because then I didn't have Mom pulling the tangles out of my bed-head. "Ow! Mom, that hurts!" I'd say whenever she tugged a comb through my hair.

"Well, hold still then!"

The best thing about Mom working was the extra cash. One evening she went to the movies with Betty. It must have been a showing of the 1953 version of *Titanic* in a theatre close by, because I remember her telling Ron and me that the movie was about an unsinkable ship that sank anyway. With Mom at the show, we watched television with Uncle Jack and had a special popcorn treat. When she came home later that night, even though we were tired, we jumped all over her because we were so thrilled she'd had a night out.

Then, on a Saturday afternoon some weeks later, she took Ron and me to our first movie, *Bambi*, an animated film, the main character being a young fawn. I remember being enchanted by the sweet animals in the forest yet tormented by the horrible fate of Bambi's mother, who was killed by a hunter. For days afterwards I held Mom's hand a little tighter and hugged her a little closer. That movie haunted me for years.

It couldn't have been too many days later that I went to the house of my friend Laura. I remember it was sometime after Ron's eighth birthday party, when we boisterous children, mainly Ron's classmates, had played Red Rover in the backyard with Uncle Jack while Mom cooked hot dogs for us. Laura, a classmate who liked to hang on the monkey bars with me, lived a short walk from the school, and I remember admiring her beautiful house—a nine—and feeling a little out of place there. It stood two storeys tall on a tidy lawn shaded by maples. All the houses in that neighbourhood were similar, all eights and nines, and even though I loved my home a mile away from the school, like its neighbours, it was only about a six.

The inside of Laura's house was even more stunning. While Laura yelled downstairs to her older brother to tell him she was home, I quickly scanned the main floor: modern plush couches, artwork on the walls, chandeliers and a large dining set beside a cabinet of glassware. After following her down the carpeted hallway, I saw that her room was the most impressive of all: a pink canopy bed with flowing sashes and frilly pillows. Against the wall stood a beautiful dollhouse, complete with miniature furniture and figurines that I could hardly wait to get my hands on.

What fun we had! I was so enthralled that I lost track of time. "I have to leave. It's getting dark," I said reluctantly, sad that our time was over. "My mom will get mad if I'm not home for dinner."

"Okay," she said. "See you tomorrow."

"Yeah, see you tomorrow." I waved as I set out to walk home alone.

I was fine at first. She lived on a quiet street, but once I got to the main intersection, I didn't feel so brave anymore. Cars and people were everywhere. I started to cry quietly as I stood waiting for the light to change. That's when a young woman with a friendly face and long hair approached me.

"Hey, little girl, is everything okay?" she asked, kneeling down to talk to me in a gentle, kind voice.

"I am … am trying to … to go home," I stuttered between sobs.

"I can give you a ride. My car is across the street," she offered generously.

"Oh, okay," I said. A ride sounded much nicer than walking, and it would be lots faster. She took my hand and walked me to her car. She was alone so I climbed into the front seat and clipped on my seat belt. Even though we didn't have a car, I'd been in my grandparents' car so I knew how to put on a seat belt.

"Do you know where you live?" she asked, turning on the ignition.

I nodded as my tears dried up, feeling better now that I wasn't alone. "Just turn around and go down that way," I said, pointing to the walking route we took to school. In a few minutes she pulled up in front of the house. "This is my place. Thank you," I said, remembering my manners.

She opened the door for me, then walked me to the front door.

Mom was smoking on the front steps, waiting for me. I'd told Ron at school to tell her where I was going so she wouldn't worry. "Hello," she said to the lady who had driven me home. "You must be Laura's mom. Thanks for driving Phyllis home."

"Oh, no," the lady said. "I saw your daughter on the street corner, and I could see she was upset so I offered to drive her home."

"Oh, okay," Mom said, confused.

"Glad to help out," the lady said and walked back to her car.

"What was all that about?" Mom said, turning to me. "Since when is it okay to take a ride from strangers?"

While later I could see the safety boundaries I had crossed, at the time I didn't understand why my mother was so mad, because I had followed her rules. After all, I was home before dinner.

━━

One morning near the end of June I opened my eyes to filtered light shining into a room that wasn't mine, and I had a feeling that things weren't as they should be. Even more odd was the fact that I was naked, which was strange because I always wore my white cotton nightgown to bed, the one with the satin bow at the top. Now I was lying tummy down and my bed didn't feel right at all. It was all lumpy and coarse, not soft and cozy. The air wasn't right either. It reeked of sweat and cigarettes. I knew I had to get ready for school, so I slowly raised my head, wiping away some drool at the side of my mouth, and saw a man's stubbly chin and a face looking at me. It was Uncle Jack's face. I went to roll off his body, but he held me close, wrapping his arms around me, holding me down, pinning me on top of him.

"No, Uncle Jack, no. Let me go!" I screamed when it dawned on me what he was up to. Mom's warnings about boys echoed in my head. *They're only after one thing, Phyllis.* I flailed at him frantically, trying to force my body off him to save myself, but it was no use. There was no way I could overpower him.

"Settle down, settle down!" he yelled, determination on his face.

"Please, Uncle Jack! Don't! Please, don't!" I begged as my tears poured.

I must have passed out from the shock, the situation too much for my young mind to handle, because the next thing I remember is waking up in the bed I shared with Mom, wearing my pink housecoat. It was as if it were a bad dream. I got up to go to the washroom as I did every morning, but when I stood to flush, I saw a white, frothy liquid floating on the surface of the toilet water, which I thought was unusual. I watched it swirl away, then got ready for school. Minutes later when Uncle Jack entered the kitchen as I ate my cereal, my whole body shrank. His hair was messy and he wore a grubby T-shirt and jeans. I just wanted to disappear, to melt into the floor.

"Give this to your teacher," he said, placing a slip of paper on the table. It was a note explaining my tardiness. Then he walked back to his room and shut the door.

I can't remember if I read the note, but I do remember that I ate quickly and left the house as soon as I could. I had to get away even though I had never walked to school alone until that day. Looking back, I realize I must have been high on adrenalin. It must have been recess or perhaps lunch break when I arrived, because children were on the playground.

Laura ran to greet me. "Hey, you're late. Everything okay?"

"Yeah, I was feeling sick, had a headache." I didn't know what else to say. I joined her on the monkey bars, swinging around and laughing as if it were a regular day. After the bell I gave my teacher the note. She read it quickly, then started the next lesson.

As it was almost the end of the school year, we were doing hands-on activities to keep us engaged while the sun shone, tempting us outside. Miss Wilson had planned an art project, pasting shapes into a collage. With my head in a fog, all I did was squish the white paste between my fingers, spread the stickiness across my desk, then watch it fall onto the carpet, my classmates a cloud of commotion around me.

"What do you think you're doing?" Miss Wilson snapped, bringing me back to reality. "Look at the mess you're making! Clean this up!"

When I arrived home, I told Mom what Uncle Jack had done. I knew. I'd heard the older kids talking at school. I'd watched television. I knew what he did was wrong. I knew I'd been his victim. Mom's warnings told me so. I also believe that by fainting, by having no memory of the actual violation, my body had reacted with a survival mechanism that saved me.

"Mom, Uncle Jack humped me," my six-year-old self said as she straightened the shoes by the door.

She stopped what she was doing and looked straight at me. "What did you say?"

Thinking she hadn't understood, I changed my wording. "Uncle Jack fucked me, Mom."

Her face tight, her lips pursed shut and her eyes wide with anger, likely in shock, rather than comfort me, she walked to the phone. "Mom, Jack raped my daughter! He raped her! That fucking asshole! Don't tell me to calm down! You don't believe me? Phyllis told me in her own words, goddammit!"

My mother was looking for support, but my grandmother couldn't believe that her son had raped her grandchild. As for her daughter, she'd seen my mother blur reality before and must have thought she was blurring it again. Distraught, my mother didn't seem to know what to do. After slamming down the receiver, she wandered aimlessly around the room, muttering under her breath, her entire body shaking. Left to my own devices, not wanting to think about the situation and finding it hard to look at my mother, I left the room and distracted myself by playing in the yard with Ron and Lorraine. Later that evening, when Jack got home, the house became a battle zone as Mom fought for me.

"WHAT DID YOU DO TO MY DAUGHTER? WHAT DID YOU DO TO HER?" Mom yelled, her face contorted by madness.

"What are you talking about?" Jack yelled back.

With all the slamming, yelling and cursing, Ron and I ran upstairs and hid beneath our covers.

When we left for school the next day, it would turn out to be our last day of the term. We would never return to that school, never see our classmates again, never say goodbye. After school, as Ron and I approached home, I didn't think much of the lingering smoky smell in the air. Perhaps a vehicle with heavy exhaust had just gone down Kingsway.

Then I was standing on the sidewalk beside my brother, looking at the place where our house used to be. It was hard to believe that only that morning I had dressed in my bedroom, eaten breakfast at the kitchen table and walked down the front steps of a house that was no longer there. All that was left of the home in the community I cherished was the concrete foundation and heaps of garbage bags on the lawn. Looking closer, I realized they weren't full of garbage. They held the charred remnants of our belongings. I saw Raggedy Ann's stripey legs, twisted and dirty, sticking out of the wreckage; my doll stroller, half melted; and soggy mattresses and blankets, including the floral comforter Mom and I had shared. Rudolph was on top of another heap, looking sad and droopy. Ron stood aghast too as he took in the piles of ruined possessions. Hearing talk coming from the garage, we ran over. Mom and Uncle Jack were standing a mile apart from each other among boxes, furniture and racks of clothes that had somehow been saved. Their faces were rigid.

"What happened?" Ron asked.

"Jack burned the house down. He was mad at me because I kicked him out."

Jack may have provided the spark, but fire had swallowed the house whole. It would be years before I saw Uncle Jack after that, because he went to prison. Oakalla Prison.

GETTING BY

"Those kids don't appreciate their toys," Mom said, eyeing our landlord's sandbox from the kitchen window as she scrubbed dishes in our basement suite. "They can't even be bothered to put them away. If they leave their toys out, you should take them. You'd appreciate them and respect them more than they do."

It was true that the boy and girl who lived upstairs, too young to be our playmates, didn't seem to care about their toys. They'd leave buckets, shovels, cars and diggers out in the pouring rain. Even so, Ron and I looked at each other anxiously, knowing that would be stealing.

"Go on!" Mom said, encouraging us. "I think they're out."

Hesitantly I followed Ron outside. I could tell he was as nervous as I was. Glancing up at the windows for movement to make sure the coast was clear, Ron quickly grabbed a yellow dump truck, and I grabbed a couple of pails and shovels. Then we ran in the door with our new toys. Mom wore a look of triumph. After that, on the odd occasion they left their toys out, we stole them. We knew better than to play with them outside where we could be seen, so we played with them indoors. Fortunately they had so many toys they didn't even seem to notice when a few of them disappeared.

I was seven now, and after seeing Laura's beautiful home, I realized how truly poor we were. My grandparents had donated furniture and clothes to replace what we'd lost in the fire, but it wasn't enough to improve our station in life, and it didn't help that Mom had quit her job. Now, whenever we went to Deer Lake, the fancy houses stood out to me more than ever. One afternoon I stood stock still in the water staring at them, mesmerized by their sheer size, imagining what a girl's bedroom in one of them might look like and picturing a pink canopy bed like Laura's with soft, flowing curtains and a beautiful dollhouse. The next thing I knew, I felt a spray of cold water. Ron had splashed me, so I turned to splash him back, laughing in the sunshine, forgetting about my lot in life.

Our home was calmer now that Uncle Jack didn't live with us. When Uncle Walter and Pat arrived at the door one day, I barely remembered them, but Uncle Walter's smile jogged my memory of playing catch that long-ago afternoon.

"Hi there," he said enthusiastically, opening the door of his black Chrysler as Ron and I stood in the doorway, Mom behind us. We smiled back, while Pat, older now, shyly looked on.

"Why don't you kids play outside?" Walter suggested.

Ron and I walked out to the yard, looking encouragingly at Pat, who wasn't too sure at first.

"It's okay," Walter said, as he entered our basement suite to chat with Mom. "They're your cousins. Go on," he said, giving his son a nudge.

Before long, Pat was following Ron around, catching bugs.

"I found some ants!" or "Hey, a spider!" Ron would say and then give the critter to Pat to hold before putting it into a glass jar. When he had quite a collection, he'd lie on the grass studying them.

"Look at this, Phyllis!" Ron would say. "There are ten ants in here with a spider. The ants are attacking the spider."

"Cool!" I'd say to keep him happy. I was more interested in my doll, the one my grandparents had given me for Christmas a couple of years earlier. I couldn't push her in the stroller anymore because it had melted in the fire, but the doll had been salvaged.

That's how the days went whenever Walter and Pat came by, which was about every couple of weeks, and it was nice for Mom to have some adult company since we didn't live beside Betty anymore. After quite a few visits, with Pat feeling comfortable around us, our uncle would even leave Pat in Mom's care for a few hours. He and Ron would hunt for bugs while I'd play house. Sometimes Mom would take the three of us to the park, where our games of tag were a lot more fun because with three of us I wasn't "it" all the time.

Most days I'd hang out with a couple of girls who were in my class at school and lived just down the street—Annie, a kind, soft-spoken girl, and Rani, who always had a bright smile. I was one of the top students in my class. My favourite subject was language arts, and I always beamed with pride when our teacher, Miss Brown, complimented my reading and spelling skills. After school we girls would meet beneath the oak tree in Annie's front yard, where we'd collect acorns and feed them to our dolls. Sometimes we'd savour the crunchy bitterness ourselves, cracking them open with our teeth.

Occasionally Jeff and Ricky, two boys from our class, would join us. Ricky, who was the leader of the two, thought he was better than everyone because of his brand-name clothes, though I didn't know what that meant back then. He was always neatly turned out in pressed jeans, brightly coloured shirts and shiny, sleek runners. I never really knew what to think of him, as he could be nice to me one day and mean the next. He was the only kid I remember who made fun of my "Sally Ann clothes."

On one of Ricky's nice days, he and Jeff wandered over with Ricky leading the way. We were making small talk when he noticed a large pile of long cedar branches in the treed lot next door.

"Hey, let's make a fort!"

"Yeah, sure! Great idea!" we replied, not wanting to disagree and cause any trouble.

"We could put the branches across those logs," Ricky suggested, pointing to two fallen trees that were about eight feet apart. We spent the next hour or so dragging branches and laying them across in rows, then crawled in to lie side by side, breathing in the cedar-and-dirt-smelling air and making comments like "cool" and "awesome." Suddenly my heart started racing. I felt trapped, the same way I'd felt when Uncle Jack had me pinned on top of him. Barely able to breathe, I knew I needed out. Fortunately I was on the outside edge, and I somehow managed to say, "I have to go home for dinner." Rolling out, I stood in the open, catching my breath before racing home.

—⚭—

Ron had a harder time fitting in at our new school than I did. At home he'd usually play by himself, arranging his green plastic soldiers into battle formations on the floor of our small rec room. Then one afternoon I found him sitting on his bedroom floor with Mom's compact mirror in one hand and a needle in the other, intently looking at his reflection and poking at his face.

"What are you doing?" I asked him.

"I'm taking my freckles off. I don't like them. Kids make fun of me."

"Oh!" I said, surprised his face wasn't covered in blood. He was using the needle carefully. I could see tiny bits of skin sticking up on his cheeks, and I was thinking that it wasn't going to work but didn't have the heart to tell him. I knew kids made fun of him. One afternoon I'd heard a boy call him a "scrawny little runt," and I wished he would stand up for himself. Part of me wanted to shout back and tell the kid off myself, but I knew that wouldn't help the situation, being his little sister. I knew it was best to ignore the stinging comment.

It didn't help that Ron was small for his age. We both were, but I think Ron was skinnier than I was. When we had baths together, I could see his ribs. While I felt I had enough to eat, I wonder now if he did, being older and taller. There was never much food around. Our fridge was half the size of the one at our grandparents' house, and it was bare most of the time. I could count the number of items in seconds. I'd see the inside when Mom prepared meals. Usually there was a jug of milk, a package of processed cheese slices, a container of Kool-Aid and a few apples. On a tight budget, Mom had to plan meals carefully. We did a big shop about every two weeks, and I remember seeing her shopping lists lying on the kitchen table. Each item had a cost beside it with a total at the bottom, which was usually around a hundred dollars.

Beans $3
Milk $3
Bread $2
Peas $1
Peanut butter $3
Fish sticks $5 ...

We did our shopping at the grocery store in the nearby mall, which was too far away to walk, so we took the bus. To pass the time, I'd either rate houses or study the bus brochure, *The Buzzer*, that Mom would often hand me to read along the way. It was all about bus routes and services.

In the store Mom would add up the cost of the items, talking out loud as she shopped. "Let's see. Three plus five is eight and four is twelve ..."

Once, Ron and I played tag around the cart, giggling, and Mom lost count. "Twelve and three is fifteen, plus another three is eighteen … no, fifteen … or is it eighteen? Would you guys be quiet?" she shouted. "I can't think! Now I have to start over!"

And she did, counting each item in the cart and getting a total before selecting more items. Looking back, I realize that thinking out loud likely helped her keep her meagre finances on track. Ron and I looked guiltily at each other. We were quiet after that. Mom always stuck to her list. We knew better than to ask for anything extra.

Because there were too many groceries for a mother with two youngsters to carry on the bus, she'd usually save just enough money for a taxi home. After the groceries were put away, she'd "make" milk. We couldn't afford milk in a carton. We got that only at our grandparents' house. Instead she'd prepare powdered milk because it was more economical. I remember standing on the other side of the kitchen one day, watching, but she was so focused on her task that I don't think she knew I was there. She followed the directions on the bag, putting the powder in the jug first. Then she added a cup of hot water from the tap, after letting the water run until it steamed. Hot water was a good choice because the powder dissolved better. After a few minutes of stirring, she added more hot water, stirring for what seemed like forever. Every once in a while she'd take a spoonful out and check it for lumps, though it was pretty much impossible to have lump-free milk. Once most of the lumps were gone, she'd fill up the rest of the jug with steaming water and place it in the fridge to cool. Later we'd have little lumps floating in our cups like miniature dumplings, and on our morning cereal there were always blobs of powdered goo, but Ron and I never complained. It was the only milk we had. We were used to it.

For school lunches, Mom would usually make either peanut butter or processed cheese sandwiches with an apple on the side. For dinner, she'd prepare just enough food for us, dividing the food evenly onto three plates. There were never seconds. If we had fish sticks, we'd have two each with whipped potatoes, which I loved because she'd use the electric beater Granny gave her to mix in milk and butter to make them creamy. And she always made sure we had our greens, usually tasteless canned peas that I hated, though she always made me eat them. She hated wasting food. To her, food was money we didn't have, though she never said as much or let on that she was a regular at the food bank. All she'd say was "Vegetables are good for you."

My favourite meal was baked macaroni. Mom made the best-tasting mac and cheese ever. After cooking the pasta, she'd stir in milk and grated cheese, then bake it in a little white casserole dish, making just enough for three. As we ate, strings of cheese would hang from our forks. When we had dessert, which wasn't often, it would be strawberry Jell-O or canned fruit cocktail. It was such a treat to get a cherry that goodness help my poor mother if there was only one in the can.

"I want the cherry!" I'd say.

"No, I do! She got it last time," Ron would complain, and we'd go on and on bickering over the rosy treasure.

"You guys, quit your arguing! I'm going to have the cherry, and that will solve the problem," Mom would say.

Now that we were a little older, Mom gave us responsibilities. "Ronnie! Phyllis! I need someone to set the table," she'd yell. Pushing the boundaries, sometimes we listened and sometimes we didn't, and the odd time she'd say, "Don't make me get out the wooden spoon!" I don't remember her ever using it, but the threat usually worked. One of us would set out the knives, forks and plastic cups, second-hand dishes from our grandparents, but they did the job.

Some evenings Mom would heat up powdered milk, which tastes better warm and steamy. "Milk helps you sleep," she'd say, serving it in mugs as we sat together at the kitchen table, sipping it slowly so as not to burn our tongues. I liked to wrap my hands around the warm mug as I drank. Often, while Mom listened, Ron and I would chatter about a show we'd watched on television. I remember we'd watched *The Jungle Book* one night, and I said something like "I like Baloo the bear best."

"Not me," Ron said. "Bagheera's my favourite!"

Then it was time to brush our teeth and get ready for bed. "Good night, Mom! See you in the morning," we'd say, sharing quick kisses.

———

That Christmas, when we gathered at my grandparents' place with Uncle Walter and his family for the annual celebration, Granny wasn't there. Nobody told me that, because my grandparents had divorced, she had moved back to Ottawa. A sparkly lady I'd never see again was sitting in the plush rocker where Granny should have been. She wore a twinkling gold necklace, silvery hoop bracelets and a pale green silky dress with a sash around the waist. She looked like an aging Egyptian princess, and she smoked like the movie stars I'd seen in the movies Mom watched on television, with a smoke dangling between her fingers. The sparkly lady would take a deep puff, pull the cigarette slowly away from her mouth, exhale a curling trail of smoke, then flash a smile of shiny white teeth.

After dinner with all the trimmings, the highlight of the evening was opening presents. They gave me a Baby Alive doll. She had blond hair and blue eyes just like Laura, the friend I never saw anymore, so that's what I named her. I carried Baby Laura everywhere, feeding her milk, changing her clothes and clipping her hair with barrettes just like the ones Mom clipped in mine.

For the next few months we kept busy with school, visits to parks or quiet days at home. Sports day at school that June was particularly memorable because, after all the fun and games in the sun, every student received a lunch of a hot dog and a single serving of milk. I remember walking eagerly toward the pink and white carton sitting on my desk waiting for me. That rich and cool, creamy milk was the most memorable part of my day. Another highlight that month was when Uncle Walter took us kids to *Star Wars*.

So life for Ron and me was happy. Normal. It wouldn't last. One day, while we were at school, our mother met with her psychiatrist. With hope for a better life, with hope to be taken seriously, with hope that she was cured, she had decided to go off her medication. The thing is—there is no cure for schizophrenia.

IDENTITY CRISIS

As much as Mom did her best to keep the place warm looking and tidy, there were no family pictures around, and I have no birth story. Mom never said, "I remember the day you were born." She never talked about her childhood either, no stories of "When I was a kid …" The only time she talked about her past was to complain about my father.

That winter, a couple of months after we'd spent Christmas with Aunt Lynn's brother-in-law and his wife, who had kindly picked us up in their station wagon since Granddad hadn't invited us over, Ron and I were entertaining ourselves in the rec room when Mom mentioned our long-lost father. Ron was pushing a dump truck he'd stolen from the sandbox, and I was sharing cake with Baby Laura. I'd used the Easy-Bake Oven my grandparents had given me before Granny moved away to bake this special treat. A few months back, I'd surprised Mom with a miniature chocolate cake on her birthday. She was so pleased when we sang birthday greetings that she even helped us find a candle. "Make a wish first, Mom! Make a wish!" we'd excitedly exclaimed while she paused momentarily to dream before we divided that little cake into three.

We had always made wishes on our birthdays. Before extinguishing the flame with my hopeful breath, I would wish for gifts like dolls or books. Now that I was older, my wishes were bigger and more important. Now I wished that the kids at school would be kind to Ron and that we weren't poor. I made sure not to tell anyone my wishes, just as Granny had instructed me years earlier, but so far none of them had been granted. Kids still made fun of Ron, and I knew we still didn't have much money. I wondered how long it would take for my wishes to come true or if they ever would.

"I just got off the phone with your dad," Mom said, walking down the hallway. I was surprised because I didn't know she was in touch with him. In fact, I thought she didn't ever want to speak to him again.

Just the other day at school, two older girls had commented on the scar on my shin. I had just come out of a stall in the washroom wearing my favourite corduroy gauchos.

"What's that mark on your leg?" the taller girl asked as I washed my hands.

"Yeah, that's quite a scar! What happened?" the other girl inquired.

I didn't tell them what I'd heard about how I got the scar. It didn't seem right. "Oh, that? It's a birthmark," I lied. "It's been there as long as I can remember." This was true.

"Wow, that's quite the birthmark," they agreed before leaving.

Now I listened intently to Mom because I was curious about this man I didn't know. I'd never even seen a picture of him. But Ron and I were both fairer than Mom. Ron had sandy-blond hair while my previously wispy blond hair had turned golden brown. I had Mom's green eyes while Ron had her smile, but his eyes were blue.

"He says he's going to send you a belated Christmas gift. I'll believe it when I see it. He never sends us anything. He just drinks his money, spends it all on booze. He's good for nothing. If you don't watch it, Ronnie, you're going to be just like him one day."

She went back to the kitchen, Ron went back to playing with his truck, and I continued eating cake with Baby Laura, wondering what my father would send—or if he would send anything at all. A couple of weeks later a parcel arrived. Our father had sent Ron fifty dollars and he'd sent me an Inuit doll. With her long, shiny black hair and thick lashes, she was the most beautiful doll I had ever seen. She wore soft leather mukluks, a leather vest with beaded tassels and a leather skirt with colourful beaded embroidery. When I laid her down in my arms, her long-lashed eyelids would close. When I stood her up again, her luscious brown eyes would reappear. As she was the only gift I had ever received from my father, I decided that she was too special to play with, and I placed her on my dresser. But Mom was right about him drinking his money. That would be the last we'd hear of him for many years.

In the meantime Ron had money to spend, and about a week later we went to Brentwood Mall. Mom and I shopped for groceries while he went to the sports store across the way. After our groceries were bagged, we found him sitting on the foyer bench where Mom had asked him to wait.

"Look what I got!" he exclaimed as we approached.

"Wow, nice hockey sticks! What's the poster?" I asked, thinking it would be a hockey player.

"Farrah Fawcett," he replied, unrolling the scroll. There she was in all her red bathing suit glory. The poster he'd purchased would become iconic.

"Cool," I said. While I was happy for him, Mom wasn't.

"What?" she said, not quite loud enough for people to turn and stare. "You got three things and Phyllis only got one!"

"But Mom, you said I could spend the fifty dollars however I wanted, so I did! I have a bit of change. Here, you can have it," he said, reaching into his pants pocket.

"I don't know about this," she said, taking the change. "It's not fair that you got more than Phyllis."

Poor Ron was feeling badly now, caught in a difficult situation.

"Well, I have to call a cab," Mom said icily before leaving to use the pay phone. When she returned, she started into Ron again. "You're going to have to return one of the hockey sticks."

"Aw, come on, Mom. It's not my fault they were on sale," Ron answered.

"Well, we'll just have to see," she said, letting the subject drop because our cab had arrived. By then I was starting to see Mom's point. It wasn't fair that Ron got three things and I got only one, so I shot him a dirty look in the car. He turned away and looked out the window. For the next few days Mom went on and on about the whole thing being unfair, and Ron didn't even use his hockey sticks because he likely felt too guilty. She didn't let the subject drop until Uncle Walter gave me a bicycle, which seemed, in her mind at least, to even things out.

I was ecstatic. My first bike! It was shiny purple with matching lavender tassels hanging from the handlebars. When Uncle Walter dropped it off, he didn't stay long because he had things to do, but he said he'd come back soon to teach me to ride. Though I was eight and a half, I'd never ridden a bike, having never owned one. A week or so later, tired of waiting for him and tired of watching kids my age biking around me, I decided to teach myself.

On a cold but clear mid-winter day, I took the bike from the garage and rolled it into the back alley. I didn't want anyone to see me fall.

Mom was inside cleaning, and Ron was taking shots with his hockey sticks, which he must have felt comfortable enough to use now. As I sat on the banana seat, I wobbled a lot at first. I got my pants caught in the chain, so I tucked them into my socks, but they came loose and got stuck again. There was just too much material, so that even when I walked, the bottoms flapped. In a feeble attempt to make them stylish, I would roll them up to create a cuff. This wasn't surprising as lately Mom had been insisting I wear Ron's old jeans. I realize now that she was getting ill and had started to view me as a boy.

After a few more tumbles and bruises, and after I'd freed my pants from the chain links I don't know how many times, so many that my pants were covered in oil, I got the momentum, and I was riding! I felt the wind in my hair and the freedom of gliding. I was the happiest girl in the world.

—⚭—

On a sunny afternoon not long after spring vacation had come and gone, we went to visit Betty, whom we hadn't seen in months. She had moved into a rundown old house—a five or maybe even a four—on Boundary Road, just off busy Hastings Street. The white paint was mouldy and peeling, and the overgrown lawn was covered in weeds. Unlike our bright, tidy place, her house was dusty and gloomy, and it didn't help that the curtains were closed, blocking out the sunshiny day. I was tempted to open them but knew that wouldn't be polite. Lorraine, now a tall, willowy teenager, was there too, but she wasn't interested in hanging out with us. Time had gone by and the connection had been lost. She came out of her room briefly to check out the scene but then went back in and closed the door.

Mom and Betty settled in the kitchen to catch up. Ron stayed with them. I wasn't interested in hanging around the adults, so I sat on the torn, weathered couch in the living room reading the Archie comics I'd found on the floor. We hadn't been there long when I heard rising voices.

"You can't talk to Ron that way," Betty said.

"I can talk to him however the heck I want. He's my son!" Mom said.

"Well, you can't talk to him like that in my house," Betty replied.

"Don't tell me what to do. Men are pigs! They're a waste of time, and Ronnie's going to be just like them!" Mom yelled. Thinking of my mother's words now, I realize how hard they must have been for my brother to hear, but decades later when we talked about that day, he told me that he knew she wasn't well and hadn't meant to hurt him.

Lorraine came out of her room looking worried and, after briefly glancing at me, headed for the kitchen. In the commotion that followed I couldn't hear what else was said, but later Ron told me that Mom had threatened Betty, who picked up the phone shortly thereafter. I stayed frozen on the couch, unsure whether to move or not. Before long there was a knock on the front door, and Betty came striding into the living room on her way to answer it. Mom walked slowly behind, her face like stone. Ron, looking bewildered, followed, while Lorraine looked on from the kitchen doorway.

A dark-haired man in a navy blue uniform stood at the door. He, Mom and Betty had a brief discussion, and a few minutes later Mom summoned Ron and me, and the three of us left with the policeman. While questions swam in my head, I assured myself that things would be okay because I knew police officers were caring and helpful.

Mom sat in the front seat of the cruiser while Ron and I sat in the back. Nobody spoke. You'd think it would be exciting for a child to be in a police car, but I wasn't excited at all. I was confused. At the station the officer led us past workers sitting at desks along a hallway of offices, one of which Mom was directed to. An official-looking man invited her to have a seat while Ron and I lingered, not knowing what to do. "It's okay," he said. "I'm just going to talk to your mom."

The dark-haired officer directed the two of us down the corridor, while we looked worriedly back toward Mom, trying to make sense of the situation. Moments later we were sitting at a long table in what must have been the lunchroom, which was about the size of a classroom. Vending machines lined the walls and police officers milled around.

"Hey, guys!" a different officer said in an overly friendly voice, as if he'd known us for years. He sat down beside us. "You hungry? I've got burgers and fries here."

Ron and I picked at the food, while he kindly tried to engage us in conversation, asking if we liked school and if we'd seen any good movies lately. Not in the mood for talking, I didn't bother to tell him we'd recently seen *Star Wars*. I just wanted my mom. I just wanted to go home. About thirty minutes later when Mom walked into the room, we ran up to her and wrapped our arms around her, relieved to be with her again. The dark-haired officer drove us home.

We never saw Betty again.

⸻

Only days later another strange thing happened. It was a sunny afternoon and we had just left a local park when Mom walked right out into six lanes of traffic on Canada Way, as if she were somebody else, not herself at all. "Mom! Mom! It's not safe. Come back!" Ron and I yelled from the sidewalk, exchanging fearful glances while the cars zooming by honked at her. She didn't even flinch. Then, while I looked on anxiously, Ron ran out when there was a slight break in the traffic, took her hand and guided her back to the safety of the sidewalk.

"Mom, you can't just walk into the road like that!"

"Yeah, Mom. You have to look both ways, remember?"

"All right, all right," she said calmly, apparently unaware of the worry she'd caused us.

⸻

A few weeks later she woke us in the middle of the night. "We need to leave," she said. "It's not safe for us to stay here." We were too tired and groggy to question her. Still in our pyjamas, we practically sleepwalked into the cab she had ordered while she directed the driver to a cheap motel, where we entered a room with orange shag carpet and two double beds. She directed Ron to sleep in the bed farthest from the door and told me to sleep in the one nearest the window, where she sat on the wide sill, a large kitchen knife beside her. She didn't even tuck us in.

When we woke the next morning, she was still sitting by the window holding the knife, and I didn't think she had slept at all. But she must have figured it was safe to go home because we returned, and life went back to normal until the end of the school year, not counting the rants about our "bloody landlords," with whom I figured she must have had a disagreement. I ignored her comments, just as I did when she'd go on about men.

⸻

A day or so later Mom announced that my hair was too long and I needed a "bowl cut." Ron and I had never heard of such a hairstyle, but she convinced us that people did it all the time. While Ron looked on sympathetically, she placed the stainless steel bowl that she used to make Jell-O on top of my head and chopped away. I watched sadly as my locks fell to the floor.

For days afterwards I had to endure finger-pointing stares at school, and one afternoon as I walked home from Annie's, Ricky made fun of my haircut. I can't remember his exact words, but I know I made a snide remark back. He could dish out the teasing, but he couldn't take it himself, and when it dawned on me what I'd done, I started to run. Unfortunately he was bigger and faster, and he caught up when I was nearly home. He tripped me, sending me flying, and I skinned my knee on the driveway.

"What happened?" Mom asked when I walked in the door, whimpering. I couldn't tell her the truth. She was so easily upset these days that I told her I had tripped, and she fixed me up with hydrogen peroxide and bandages.

———

Our summer holidays started on a bright morning filled with the promise of something new and exciting. While we ate our cold cereal, Mom asked, "Ronnie, Phyllis, how about we go on a ferry?" Complimentary rides were being offered to celebrate the grand opening of the SeaBus that would transport walk-on passengers back and forth across Burrard Inlet between downtown Vancouver and the North Shore.

"Cool! Yay! Let's go on the ferry!" we exclaimed.

"Well, you better get ready," Mom said, and she began packing a lunch.

As it was a lovely day, I put on shorts, a T-shirt and a light jacket, thankful that for once Mom hadn't insisted I wear Ron's old clothes. As the bus approached our stop in the city core, the day was already so hot that I had to peel my legs off the seat before getting off. We walked the long, windowed skywalk to the waiting area, admiring the city view and the ocean sparkling like diamonds.

"Here it comes! It's coming!" Ron and I exclaimed as the Sea-Bus approached. Once aboard, we walked quickly to the front, Mom following, and there we knelt on the seats with Mom between us to look out the expansive windows. While seagulls squawked overhead, we took in the view of the apartment buildings and barges along the opposite shoreline, then stayed aboard as the ferry made the return trip. About a quarter of an hour after we'd docked again in Vancouver, Mom suggested we go again because the ride was so short.

"Yeah, yeah, let's go!" we replied enthusiastically, running ahead to get in line.

By about the fourth time back and forth across the harbour, the novelty had worn off, but Mom insisted we keep riding even after we'd eaten our sandwiches. We'd disembark, wait for the next SeaBus, then embark again to sail back.

"Can't we go home now, Mom?" we pleaded.

"Nope. We're not going home." She was being unreasonable, but who were we to argue with our mother? To and fro we went.

"The ferry's here, Mom. Time to get on," Ron said in a tired voice after we'd been riding the ferry for hours.

"Nope. I'm not getting on. Someone has taken my children and I want them back," Mom said, her expression frozen, and she sat down on a bench against the wall.

Ron and I looked at each other with the same question on our faces. *What is she talking about?*

I gave it a try. "Mom! It's time to go. The SeaBus is here."

"No," Mom said. "I want my kids back."

People were starting to stare at us. Ron and I were flabbergasted, not to mention worried. I know now that our mother's brain was deep into a psychotic episode.

"Mom, it's me. I have your eyes, green eyes just like yours. Look, look! It's really me. It's Phyllis!" my schoolgirl voice said, trying to convince her, but she just stared ahead and didn't move a muscle.

"Yeah, Mom," Ronnie said, flashing a huge grin.

No response.

"Look at my smile," he said. "This is *my* smile. It's Ronnie!"

Everybody else had boarded now, and one of the SeaBus attendants, a tall fellow with a white shirt and navy blue pants, came by. "Ma'am, you need to get on the ferry now or you're going to miss it."

"I'm not moving until I get my kids back."

There was no reasoning with her. All we could do was cry, "Mom, it's us! It's really us! We *are* your kids," as our tears fell. Mom didn't respond. It was as if we weren't even there.

Whenever an attendant came by to try to persuade her to board, she wouldn't move, insisting that someone had taken her real children. She just stared ahead while Ron and I slept at her feet, crying intermittently as we watched crowds of people come and go, children holding their parents' hands or being pushed in strollers. I wondered if we'd ever go home.

As dusk approached and yet another boarding cleared away, Ron and I were exhausted. That was when two police officers arrived and managed to persuade Mom to move from the bench she'd planted herself on. But instead of taking the SeaBus, we rode in uncomfortable silence with one of the officers in his cruiser. Once again Mom sat in the front, while Ron and I sat in the back.

As I looked out the window at the city lights shining brightly in the darkness, I felt nothing. I was a robot. The police officers took us to the same police station we had gone to the last time. One fellow talked to Mom in a closed room, while another brought Ron and me burgers and fries in the lunchroom and tried to engage us in friendly conversation. I know he was trying to make us feel better, but it didn't help. A while later the officer drove us all home.

The next day Mom and I got into an argument. I was tired of wearing Ron's hand-me-downs, and I especially hated the haircut she'd given me. "I look like a boy, Mom! I'm not a boy! I'm a girl!"

She didn't like what I had to say and surprised me when she yelled, "Fine, then, leave! I've had enough of you anyway!"

I was shocked because I knew she loved me. How could she be so mean? Maybe she just meant "Get out of this room." Maybe she meant "Get out of my sight," but no matter, I left. I'd had enough of her too. I grabbed Baby Laura, slammed the door behind me as I left the house and walked down the street clutching the doll to my chest, thinking that by running away, I'd teach her a lesson.

I walked and walked and walked, and after a time I found myself walking beside four lanes of traffic along Canada Way, and that's when a slim lady not much older than my mother approached me. She was wearing heels, a streamlined grey jacket and a matching skirt. She asked where I was going, and I told her I'd had an argument with my mother and that I was running away.

"I'm sorry to hear that," she said. "But I think I can help. Come with me."

I didn't give it a second thought. She seemed friendly. I took her hand and walked with her into a nearby building, a place that seemed familiar. Once I walked through its doors, I realized I was in the police station. Again.

—∞—

All these years later, I have learned that it was those many weeks without medication that caused the delusions and hallucinations of paranoid schizophrenia to wreak havoc in our mother's brain, compounded by anosognosia, the inability to recognize a relapse. But as far as I can tell from reading her records, not one mental health professional had kept our vulnerable little family on the radar during that entire time. As for our parent-child relationship, Mom's psychiatrist actually stated for the record, "The last child I evaluated was in 1964, and I have been out of the evaluation of parent-child interaction and suitability for more than a decade, and I really don't consider myself qualified in that area of psychiatry." Unbelievable.

House of Strangers

I had shown my mom, all right. Now I was like a leaf being tossed around with no choice where to land. I spent the rest of that day inside dull offices with ladies directing me. This way, Phyllis. Stay here, Phyllis. Come with me, Phyllis. Tell us what happened, Phyllis. I can't remember how many there were, but one lady had blond hair, and another was older with greying hair. I realize now that they were social workers, but back then I'd never heard of a social worker. I answered their questions. I wasn't shy. I told them that my mother had lost her temper, that we'd gone to a motel in the middle of the night, that she believed Ron and I weren't her children and that we rode the SeaBus all day. I even showed them the scar on my leg. They'd nod, smile and frown, talking to each other in low voices at times, shaking their heads at my mother's behaviour as they took notes at a table, their briefcases beside them.

Next thing I knew, the blond lady was parking her car in front of a large white house with brown trim. "Well, this is the place where you'll be staying for a while," she said. Mom had said it was not okay to take rides from strangers, yet here I was about to live with strangers.

The house was an eight or a nine with a bright flower bed along the front and a deep green lawn. I glanced at the large, modern homes nearby and their perfectly manicured lawns. They were all eights and nines. An older lady with mousy brown hair streaked with grey answered the door.

"Oh, yes, come in, come in," the lady said, looking down at me. "We've been expecting you. Why don't you go into the playroom? There's a little girl about your age there who would love to meet you. It's at the top of the stairs on your right."

Leaving the ladies on the landing, I climbed the stairs and looked down into the living room, where I saw floral couches and rich, dark wooden tables and chairs similar to the furniture in my grandparents' house. A stocky, gruff-looking stranger with white hair was reclining on one of the couches, his feet up on a stool. He was engrossed in a newspaper. Turning to the right, I saw a girl sitting on the floor of a room, playing with the most beautiful dollhouse I'd ever seen, even more beautiful than Laura's. It was almost as tall as I was with multiple floors, many rooms and miniature people and furniture. As I entered, I couldn't help but glance into a side room that held a massive bed with wooden tables on each side and a matching dresser.

The girl was short and squat and had chubby fingers, a plump, gentle face, thick red lips and deep-set eyes that were placed close together. When she spoke, her tongue seemed too large for her mouth and her words were unclear, but I listened intently and figured out her name was Taya, though it came out as "Yaya." After I introduced myself, she called me "Lillis."

In the days that followed, I spent every waking moment with her. Usually we played with the dollhouse, but sometimes I'd read to her from the shelf of children's books against the wall. With the exception of school and the public library, I'd never seen so many books in one place. I'd put Baby Laura in my lap or, as Taya was such a gentle girl, I'd let Laura sit in her lap, then we'd sit side by side on the floor, enjoying stories like *Winnie-the-Pooh* and *Clifford the Big Red Dog*. Even though she seemed to be about my age, she didn't know how to read, so I pointed to the words just as Mom had done for me.

At dinnertime the spread on the table was like the meals at my grandparents' house: dishes of roast beef, potatoes and vegetables. That first evening, sitting at the large dining room table, I politely asked, "Please pass the potatoes."

"Father!" the stocky stranger said sternly. "You call me Father and you call her Mother." He gestured toward his wife.

I reluctantly did as I was told, as "Father" had a loud and scary voice. "Pass the potatoes, please, Father," I said dutifully, forcing the words from my mouth. That's how it was each mealtime, which was a mixed blessing. Now I had all the food I could ever want, but I had to call these strangers "Mother" and "Father."

Every day was the same. Even though the weather was warm, dry and inviting, Taya and I didn't play in the yard but spent all our time in the playroom, interrupted only by meals, until it was time for bed. Taya slept upstairs just down the hall from "Mother" and "Father," but

I had to sleep in the basement in one of two single beds there. The first night, after I'd brushed my teeth in the adjoining washroom with the toothbrush these strangers had given me and put on the nightgown the blond lady had dropped off for me, and after "Mother" had bid me good night, I found it hard to sleep alone in this vast, dark room with shadows I didn't recognize. I had never felt so alone. I'd always had Mom, Granny or Ron with me. I fell asleep at last with Baby Laura clutched to my heart.

Shortly before bedtime a couple of days later, my brother arrived. I was so happy to see him, especially since I wouldn't be alone in that dark basement anymore. I wanted to run to him and give him a hug but felt reserved among these strangers, so I held back and sent him a smile instead. That night I fell asleep more quickly, knowing Ron was with me.

The following morning I woke to the smell of urine. Ron had wet the bed, something he'd never done before that I knew of.

Lady Stranger was not pleased. "You stupid idiot child! Get those wet sheets off the bed *now!*"

Staring at the floor, Ron moved slowly off the mattress. Feeling badly for him, I sent him a compassionate look, a silent apology for Lady Stranger's cruel behaviour. He nodded, then walked slowly toward the wet bed. As I walked upstairs where Lady Stranger had directed me, I could still hear her yelling. Later, when Ron joined Taya and me in the playroom, he did puzzles alone, anxiously chewing on his shirt collar.

Over the days that followed, the routine was wake up, listen to Lady Stranger yell at Ron, eat breakfast, then go to the playroom with Taya. After what seemed like a month, but really was only a week, the blond lady came back and took us away from that horrid place.

—∞∞—

It wasn't until I was writing these pages that I asked my brother where he had been during those first few days I lived alone with the strangers, and he told me that he hadn't initially come with me because they hadn't wanted to take in a boy. He had believed nobody wanted him. The social workers couldn't find another place for him, so until the strangers had a change of heart, he stayed with a couple of the police officers who had come to know us from our recent run-ins. That's all he would tell me. He said it was too hard to talk about. Looking back, I realize how different it would have been if Granny had still been around to offer support as she'd done in the past. Staying with her surely would have been much kinder.

Wards of the Court

The blond lady directed Ron and me to sit beside her on a bench in a hallway. On one side of us was a set of double doors, and on the other side was an open foyer with windows and the front door where we'd entered. Men in suits and women in smart dresses walked past us and up some stairs nearby. I can still hear the scuff of their shoes, the click of their heels and the murmurings as these people chatted. After a few minutes, the double doors opened and a uniformed man directed us into a large room filled with people, some standing in front of a row of benches and others in chairs tucked under tables. All the seats faced a cloaked, white-haired man who sat in a wooden, regal-looking chair at the front of the room. Uncle Walter was there at one of the tables.

"Uncle Walter!" Ron and I shouted, glad to see a familiar face.

"Hi, guys!" he said happily, giving us hugs. "You're going to come with me, okay?"

"Okay! Okay!" we exclaimed.

I thought he was going to take us home to see Mom. Instead, he took us to his newly purchased rancher on a quiet, suburban street in Surrey. With its perfectly manicured lawn and large bay windows, I would have given the house an eight. It just needed flowers for colour. Unlike my mother, both my uncle and Stacy were employed; in time I would discover that he had previously worked for Revenue Canada, but now he worked as a loans officer for a bank, while Stacy worked as an insurance agent.

"Well, this is our place," Uncle Walter said warmly as we followed him through the front room to the kitchen, where a tall, slim lady was puttering. "You remember your aunt Stacy, don't you?"

"Hi," she said cheerfully, looking up briefly through her modern glasses as she put away pots and pans. I only remembered meeting her once before, so I nodded and smiled shyly. Pat came running down the hall then to see what was going on.

"I'll show you to your rooms," Uncle Walter said. "This is where you'll be sleeping, Phyllis." I put my small bag of clothes in the corner by the window next to a sleeping bag on a foam mat. "Pat, show Ronnie his bed."

Later that night after Pat had gone to bed, Uncle Walter called Ron and me into the living room, where we sat on plush white couches while Aunt Stacy looked on. According to the Ministry of Children and Family Development documents that I accessed in March 2016, the blond social worker had apparently suggested that Walter tell us our mother was "still ill in hospital" and our return to her depended on "her getting better." Her report said, "In case they are feeling guilty, [he should] reassure them that her hospitalization isn't their fault." She went on to write that Uncle Walter was "anxious" to have us. "He has often been concerned about the kind of parenting they were receiving from Carolyn," her report said. When I read this years later, it occurred to me that he couldn't have found her parenting too terrible as he'd left Pat in her care on several occasions. But all he said to us that night was "You'll be staying with us for a while. If you like, you can call us Mom and Dad. I'll be bringing the rest of your clothes and belongings over tomorrow." Just as when we had lived with the strangers, calling Walter and Stacy Mom and Dad wouldn't have felt right to me at all. While I didn't understand why we couldn't see our mother, I did realize that the crowded room we had been taken to earlier that day was a courtroom and a decision had been made there: we couldn't live with our mother anymore. And a voice in my head told me, *This is all your fault. This is because you ran away.*

⸺

We didn't see Mom at all that summer, but those first nights at Walter and Stacy's were the hardest. As I lay among the dolls and stuffed animals I'd accumulated over the years, I pined for my mother. In the evenings Walter read to us kids from the novel *Jonathan Livingston Seagull*, a fable about a seagull who was exiled from his clan but was able to soar anyway. Of course, I didn't understand the moral back then, but when the story was done, Walter told us that, like Jonathan, everyone in the world is special.

"How, Walter?" I asked him. "How are we special?"

"Well, let's see," he said, mulling over my question. "Ron's special because he's the oldest in the family, Pat's special because he's the youngest, and you're special because you're the only girl."

I see now that he was trying to tell us that each one of us was unique. At the time, his words left me confused because I knew Pat was my cousin, not my brother.

Not long after we'd settled into Walter and Stacy's house, there was a summer storm. Scared, I woke to a clap of thunder as flashes of lightning lit up my room. If I had been sleeping with Mom as I had done for as long as I could remember, I could have snuggled up to her. So, in the hope of hunkering down with my aunt and uncle, I rolled out of bed and quietly tiptoed down the hall in the darkness. *Knock, knock, knock,* I tapped on the door. No answer, so I tapped again.

"Yes?" Uncle Walter called groggily.

"Can I sleep with you?" I pleaded. I heard low murmuring as he whispered to Aunt Stacy.

"It's just a thunderstorm, Phyllis. Go back to bed. You'll be fine."

Disappointed, I felt my way back through the darkness and hid under my covers, turning to Baby Laura for comfort.

———

Although I thought about Mom a lot, it was easier not to think of her during the day. Sometimes Ron and I would ask when we'd see her, but Walter and Stacy never gave us a straight answer.

"Soon," they'd say. "Why don't you go play?"

Fortunately we loved to be outdoors. We'd help Walter with the yard work, which didn't feel like work at all. If he mowed the grass, we'd help rake the clippings into piles. Blackie, the family dog, who looked like a Lab but, Walter said, was a "Heinz 57," would join in, stopping now and then to lick our faces as he ran around the yard in circles. "Look, he's giving us kisses," we'd say, and Walter would laugh. Even though we walked Blackie when we could, that dog had a lot of energy. He'd often dig under the fence and get out of the yard. While he was gentle with people and loved us to stroke him and rub his belly, he wreaked havoc with other dogs.

"'S that your dog?" a man asked Walter one day as he was working in the yard while we kids played.

"Why?" Uncle Walter asked.

"Well, he's running around the place getting into all sorts of trouble. He got into a scrap with my dog. He should be on leash!"

"Well, it takes two to tango," Walter replied.

"You just make sure you keep that dog tied up!" the man replied.

When I asked Walter about it, worried because Blackie would often come home with tufts of fur hanging off him, he said, "Dogs get into scraps. It's normal, nothing to worry about." And he whistled as if he hadn't a worry in the world.

He was an amazing whistler and could whistle practically any tune. He could play tunes with his hands too—making a "loon call," he called it. I remember Ron, Pat and me sitting with him on the porch one day while he showed us how to cup our hands together to make a hollow space and then blow through them, using our thumbs as a mouthpiece and moving our fingers up and down to change the notes. We did our best, but all the sound we could muster was the air we breathed. I did learn to do the loon call eventually but could never play the melodies Walter could.

Now that I was sandwiched between two boys, I became a tomboy to fit in, joining Ron and Pat in games of street hockey with the neighbourhood kids. As long as you had a stick, you could play, and everybody had a stick. Names were passed around, teams were made up, and the game was on. Sticks smacked, the ball bounced, and kids cheered "Goal!" as the ball rolled into a cheap plastic net. Whenever a vehicle came down the street, we'd yell, "Car!" Someone would move the net to the side until it passed, then we'd resume play.

We played hide-and-seek in the meadow at the end of the road too. We'd crawl around in the dry, scratchy grass as tall as I was in an effort not to be found. Sometimes we'd find garter snakes and catch their wriggling bodies, holding them by their tails or just below their heads before releasing them and watching them wiggle away.

One afternoon a boy named Robby from down the street came by. His place was a regular meeting spot for kids because he had a trampoline.

Stacy answered the door. "Phyllis, there's someone looking for you." I put down my Archie comic and walked to the door.

"You want to come jump on the trampoline?" he asked.

"Sure. I won't be too long, Stacy."

As we walked across the yard to the street, he said, "Wow, your mom's pretty. Why do you call her Stacy?"

A feeling of alarm washed over me. I didn't want the whole world to know that I lived with my aunt and uncle. I decided to ignore his question, to pretend I never heard it. Running down the quiet street, I yelled, "You coming?"

The distraction worked. He ran to catch up with me, and we bounced on his trampoline all afternoon, the topic of my mother forgotten. From that day on, if any kids happened to be around, I was careful not to address my aunt and uncle as anything. That way I didn't have to explain why Ron and I were the only kids I knew who didn't live with at least one of their parents.

Another afternoon, after I'd been reading for quite a while and was looking for something else to do, I decided to visit Lisa, the girl next door, who was my age but a lot taller. I found her igniting rags in an abandoned van in her yard. After setting them aflame with a lighter, she'd toss them around, giggling until the burning embers faded. I hadn't forgotten that I'd lost my house to fire and wasn't interested in her dangerous game, so I retreated back to my book.

A few weeks later the top floor of her family's house burned right off. I remember standing on the street with the family and other neighbours watching it burn, flames leaping up to the sky and grey smoke filling the air as firefighters did their best to contain it, and I couldn't help but think she had something to do with it. "Such a shame," the neighbours exclaimed as the family stood quietly huddled together. Afterwards construction workers came by to clean up what was left, salvaging the bottom floor so that the family lived in a flat-roofed, single-storey house from then on.

———

In August Walter and Stacy took us camping. The first evening, after we kids had helped Walter set up the tent while Stacy set up the cookstove to start dinner, Walter showed us how to start a fire. We were happy to scurry around the shady forest collecting the moss Walter called "old man's beard" off the branches we could reach, along with dried sticks to use as kindling. The experience reminded me of the camping trip with Mom a while back, and I wished she could have joined us.

We kids looked on in wonder as, placing a good pile of moss in the middle of the firepit along with newspaper, Walter explained, "You need three components to start a fire: fuel, oxygen and heat. Help me put the moss and newspaper in the middle," he said, turning to Ron, who pulled his shoulders back, eager to follow Walter's instructions. "Don't crumple the paper too tight. Now stand the sticks loosely on top like a teepee. Make sure to leave room for oxygen, as air gives the fire energy."

"Like this?" Ron asked, trying to get the sticks to lean on one another so they'd stay up.

"Yep, that's right. Now all we need is heat. Where are the matches?"

Pat was quick to grab the matchbox off a stump and happy to pitch in. After Walter showed us how to strike a match, holding it over the fire, Ron gave it a shot. After a couple of tries, he ignited the newspaper, and moments later the kindling sticks were crackling and popping. While Pat and I jumped up and down, all giddy, Walter patted Ron on the back before adding log rounds to the fire. "Good job!" he said, and Ron beamed.

When Granny came all the way from Ottawa to visit, we told her about the camping trip.

"We got to sleep in a tent!" Ron said.

"Yeah, and we heard a bear by our campsite!" I added.

"Wow, sounds pretty scary," she said, smiling warmly.

"I wasn't scared," Pat said.

"What do you mean?" Ron said. "Of course, you weren't scared! You were sleeping!" And Pat hung his head sheepishly. Amazingly he had slept through all the commotion with Blackie barking, Stacy yelling and Walter banging pots and pans to scare the animal away.

"Yeah, and we caught trout too! Walter took us on the lake in the canoe," I said.

Before our camping trip we had been taking weekly canoe lessons at the rec centre, but I'll never forget sitting in the hard bottom of that canoe out on the lake for days before we caught anything. To pass the time, I'd made silly comments like "My butt hurts" and "My feet are dirty." I repeated myself so often that Walter teased me for days afterwards. "Are your feet dirty, Phyllis?" he'd ask, a twinkle in his eye. "How about your bottom?" Stacy had stayed at the campsite, relaxing with her

Harlequin Romance and glass of wine, but she was as pleased with our catch as we were and pan-fried the fillets in butter on the Coleman stove. I discovered that fresh trout tasted way better than fish sticks.

"And we saw stars, a whole sky of them!" Ron added. "Walter showed us the Big Dipper and the North Star."

"It certainly sounds like you had a good time," Granny said, grinning.

She was still the spry lady I remembered, and for the rest of the afternoon, after performing a series of somersaults on the spongy grass of the backyard, she showed us how to do a headstand and gave us a quarter for each one we accomplished, which was tricky to do with Blackie interrupting our concentration by licking our faces and causing us to collapse in a fit of giggles.

Then, while our gymnastics continued on the grass, Granny settled in a deck chair on the porch to talk to Walter. I couldn't make out every word of their conversation, but I heard her say, "That's great that you were able to take the kids," and I pounced on the opportunity to run over and ask, "Will we be seeing Mom soon?"

"Pretty soon," Granny answered, before Walter changed the subject as he did every time Mom was mentioned.

"Hey, why don't you guys cool off under the sprinkler?" he said. "I'll set it up."

To our delight, even Blackie ran through the water. There was no further mention of Mom, not for weeks.

In fact, our mother was demanding that Ron and I be returned to her. A report written at the time by the blond social worker and a psychologist colleague said, "As related to the topic of her children, she seems to go berserk." (Now a mother myself, I'd go berserk too if my kids were taken away.) On another occasion, when our social worker accompanied the psychologist to see our mother at a mental health clinic, our mother told them, "If they adopt my kids, I'll kill myself." Our social worker wrote that our mother "acknowledged understanding that [they] were not acting on *her* behalf." In fact, they were there to act on behalf of Ron and me; yet, with such a cold, uncaring response to our troubled and ill mother, as far as I'm concerned, they weren't representing us either. Ron and I needed and wanted our mother to be alive and well. She was in a dark place and needed compassion, not comments that brushed her off.

VISITATIONS

"Ron! Ron! Mom's here!" I yelled to my brother. With summer come and gone, it was hard to believe it was really our mother who had rung the doorbell, but there she was, standing on the landing in blue polyester pants, a camel-coloured coat and the beehive hairstyle she preferred since she had grown her hair long over the past few years.

"Well, I missed your birthday, so I thought I'd drop off a present," she said, giving me a big grin and handing me a plastic shopping bag containing a coral-coloured stuffed monkey.

"Thanks, Mom," I said and gave her a hug. I'd recently turned nine, and Walter and Stacy had given me a book on horses as I was going through a horse phase, and they knew I loved to read.

"Mom!" Ron exclaimed, entering the living room followed by Pat, whom we watched regularly after school or whenever Walter and Stacy were running errands as they were that day.

"Well, I haven't seen you two in a while. What have you been up to?" she asked, stepping inside. While Pat looked on curiously, she settled on the couch to listen as Ron and I told her about playing hide-and-seek in the tall, grassy meadow down the street.

"You've never met Blackie, have you, Mom?" Ron asked after a few minutes of catching up. "Hey, watch this!" he said, and we took turns tossing a tennis ball for Blackie while Mom laughed. Before long, she announced it was time to go.

"When will we see you again?" we asked, disappointed that she couldn't stay longer.

"Soon," she said, embracing us. "I have a bus to catch."

"We could walk with you to the bus stop," I suggested.

"That's probably not a good idea. Better that you stay here inside the house."

"Okay," I replied, my eyes watering. Ron and I waved to her through the front window. She stopped briefly to light a cigarette, then looked at the ground before walking on down the street in her slow, familiar gait. We watched longingly until she turned the corner. Gone.

When Walter and Stacy returned, we told them that Mom had come by. I thought they'd be happy we'd seen her, but Walter barely reacted and Stacy looked worried. Apparently, by dropping by, our mother had broken the guidelines. She wasn't even supposed to know where Walter and Stacy lived, and Granny must have told her when they would be out. She never came by again.

Some weeks later Stacy announced, "Phyllis and Ron, I am going to take you to see your mom after school tomorrow." Thrilled with this news, I made sure to dress nicely. Just before the new school term started, Stacy had taken us clothes shopping, and as I'd never received so many new clothes at once before, it was very exciting. She bought me a new jumper, slacks, Mary Janes, a white blouse, a brown tweed skirt and, my favourite, a skirt and matching vest covered in what looked like forget-me-nots.

"So you like your new clothes?" Stacy had asked when we left the store.

"Oh, yes. Thanks, Aunt Stacy."

"I like my baseball glove the best," Ron announced as we drove home, talking enthusiastically about our purchases.

The blond lady was waiting for us in the foyer of the building. Apparently a mental health nurse had told her earlier that our mother "had hostile feelings toward Stacy"—a natural reaction, I would think—so we left Stacy seated in the waiting area while Ron and I followed her to her office, where our mother stood to greet us.

"Mom, Mom!" we exclaimed, running toward her for a hug.

"Look at my new skirt, Mom. Isn't it beautiful?" I said, twirling so she could have a good look while she made a fuss of my hair, which wasn't styled with barrettes the way she liked.

"Do you like my new baseball glove, Mom?" asked Ron, who hoped to play ball in the spring. He and Uncle Walter played catch in the backyard.

At first Mom smiled. Then her expression changed. "Oh, sure! I'm on skid row and got my shoes at the Sally Ann for a buck while you kids are living real good," she said angrily.

I didn't know whether to feel happy or guilty. She had been fine when she'd dropped by the house to see Ron and me, but now she didn't seem fine at all.

Looking back, I realize our mother was like a wild animal on defence that day. Seeing and hearing about a financial situation she viewed as unjust had triggered the same strong emotions that had apparently erupted just weeks earlier when she had met with our blond social worker and the psychologist at the mental health centre. According to her medical records, these two had made fun of our mom, peppering her with leading, unnecessary questions so often that she had become agitated. When she had attempted to get away from them by walking to another room, they followed her as if it were some kind of game. Later, a mental health nurse had told them they had "badgered" my mother. (I could hug that woman today.) How hard it must have been for our mother to be once again in the same room as these unfeeling women, who, as far as I can tell, looked upon her with scorn.

Ron and I went quiet for a few moments. In an attempt to change the subject, I said the cream-coloured shoes she was wearing looked good on her.

Not appearing to hear me, she asked the blond lady, "How did they get all this stuff?"

"Stacy and Walter get a clothing allowance of $250 for them," she replied.

"What? Why didn't I get money for their clothes while I was on social assistance?" Mom demanded.

Awkward silence. Mom glared at the blond woman, then dug into her purse and lit up a smoke. To cheer her up, while Ron played with cars, I cooked a fish dinner at the play kitchen in the corner. I knew Mom liked fish sticks. "Here, Mom," I said, offering the meal on a plastic plate. She said I was a good cook. Just minutes later the blond lady announced it was time to leave, and Ron and I cried.

Weeks went by before we saw our mother again. This time the older, grey-haired social worker sat writing at a table while we visited. It was great to see Mom, but she seemed torn, in conflict with herself.

"Well, if I get you guys back," she said, "I don't know how I can take care of you. I can't afford fancy clothes or a nice house."

I felt bad for my mother, and my young mind decided we didn't live with her anymore because she couldn't afford to take care of us, the worry and stress being too much for her. When our social worker handed us off to a lady with short-cropped hair (the psychologist we had apparently seen twice before) for another meeting regarding our mother and our foster situation, I wanted to make everything better. This time, when she asked about our mother, school and any activities we were taking part in, I told her we went to a babysitter's after school and that I was a fairy in Brownies. "We're the fairies, glad and gay, helping others every day," I sang. "When we go back to Mom, I can cook! I can make orange juice, toast and porridge," I said eagerly as she smiled and took notes.

Years later, when I had access to those notes, I discovered she had written that our mother "must have given something to her children in spite of her own disturbance. Both are well-mannered, well-behaved and able to relate to each other and to adults. … In the ensuing weeks their anxiety level has dropped notably. … Both are more confident since finding security and acceptance with their new foster parents. Phyllis appears to be self-assured, but her confidence is quite fragile and could be adversely affected by loss of approval by any source."

———

A couple of weeks later I was promoted to sixer, leader of my Brownie pack, but I didn't want the position. I didn't deserve it. I had the fewest number of badges, and the only ones I had were the ones we earned as a group, like for crafts and art. I told myself I didn't care about silly badges, that I didn't even care about Brownies. All Brownies did was leave wrinkles in my heart. Every Tuesday evening when we met for Brownies, I was reminded of what I'd lost and what I didn't have. I remember another sixer named Suzie, who attended a school on the other side of the neighbourhood, strutting around the community hall in her Mary Janes and full sash as if she owned the place. She would smugly tell her clique of friends, all with their well-adorned sashes, about the latest badge she had earned. "I'll be getting my cooking one soon! I made spaghetti and my mom gave me this great cookbook!" They'd all congratulate her, then another girl would pipe up, "I'm getting my knitting badge next! My grandmother just gave me a basket of yarn."

I hid my jealousy of what I perceived to be their perfect families. Instead, on the sidelines, I'd talk to Natasha, whose sash was modestly full. She was in my class, liked the maypole as much as I did and sometimes invited me to play Barbies at her place. It seemed that every girl I knew had a Barbie. I'd hear their exclamations in class or on the playground: "I got a Disco Barbie for my birthday!" But what I liked most about Natasha was that she rolled her eyes whenever Suzie and her clique talked about their wonderful, silly badges.

Brownies was, however, better than baseball, which Walter and Stacy had initially signed me up for. I don't know what they were thinking. Ron was the baseball fan, not me. That first day of practice—which would be my last—the coach gave us a quick lesson on grounders and then arranged the play. My position was outfield. As I stood among the other girls with the batter ready to strike, I willed the ball not to come my way, and it didn't the first few hits. Next thing I knew, the ball was bouncing and rolling toward me, and my heart was beating like a pounding drum. I put down my glove to stop it, but I missed. All the players groaned, and one girl turned to me in disgust. "How could you miss that? It was such an easy grounder!"

That was all the encouragement I needed to quit. Fighting back tears, I marched to the car and slammed the door. "What do you think you're doing? Get back out there!" Stacy yelled. Nope. I was done.

⟶

As the Christmas season approached, Stacy dove right into the role of costume designer when she discovered that Ron, Pat and I were to be on display for the settler-themed concert at school. We were happy to leave it to her because Pat was too young to care, I would rather read and I knew Ron would rather play street hockey than spend time dressing like a pioneer. I stood beside her in my room while she knelt on the floor rummaging through my dresser, determined to find something suitable.

"What about this long skirt, Phyllis? You could pair it with this beige shirt and borrow my apron."

"Sure," I said, feigning interest while she went to fetch her apron from the kitchen.

"Put it on!" she said. "I'm going to find something for the boys."

A quarter of an hour later, they emerged in plaid shirts and dungarees. Ron's costume was finished off with a cowboy hat while Pat donned a straw one that I think Stacy found among his collection of toys. "Let's show Walter!"

Feeling silly in our getups, we lined up in the living room, where Walter was watching hockey on television. "They look great, Mom!" he exclaimed, while Stacy beamed. A week later she took pictures of our performance.

—∞—

I was hoping to see Mom for Christmas. She never appeared, but the excitement of gifts helped me forget my worries about her loneliness. Ron, Pat and I woke early that morning to open our stockings, which Santa had filled with chocolates, trinkets and a Christmas orange to keep us engaged until Walter and Stacy got up and we could open the mound of presents under the tree.

"A new Hot Wheels car!" exclaimed Pat, racing it around the floor.

Ron was thrilled with his hockey cards. "Tiger Williams! That's the one I wanted!"

And I was pleased with a necklace that I figured would look nice with my new blouse and skirt. Before long Walter emerged in a jolly mood wearing an elf hat, and Stacy settled cheerily on the couch. After an hour or so of flying paper, boxes and exclamations, I hid my disappointment that I hadn't got what I wanted—a Barbie. Even though they knew that's what I wanted, as I had talked about it all the times I'd played with Natasha, they gave me a set of miniature dolls, a perfect nuclear family of a mother, father, brother and sister, all with squat bodies and practical clothes.

"Do you like them?" Stacy asked. "They're realistic."

"If Barbie was real, she'd wear a double-D bra, have a twenty-two-inch waist and stand over six feet tall. No woman looks like that!" Walter said. Even though I knew they were trying to make a point about body image, I was disappointed. All I could think was that I was the only girl I knew of who didn't own a Barbie.

Finally one afternoon the grey-haired lady brought Mom to the house! While Stacy proudly filled them in on our school concert and the wonderful costumes she had created, Mom only glared.

In the midst of us showing her our gifts, suddenly she said, "Santa was mean to me this year. He wasn't nice."

"Maybe it's because you smoke, Mom," Ron said. "Smoking is bad for you. Maybe that's why Santa didn't bring you anything. You should quit."

"I'm not going to live long anyway so what the hell."

While I was wondering if my mother was going to die, Stacy offered her a cookie.

"Not so close," Mom said. "Stay at least two feet away from me."

I was baffled. That's when her escort suddenly stood up, grabbed her case and said it was time to go. This, according to the documents I obtained, was the rule: if our mother's behaviour wasn't stable or became unkind, visits would end.

"Well, I guess that's it then, kids," Mom said. "I don't know when I'm going to see you again. Maybe never. Looks like you don't need me anymore. You're doing better without me. I might as well move back to Ottawa."

"No, no, please don't leave," we pleaded, distraught.

"Well, we'll see. I don't know what I'm going to do."

Like my mother, I was torn. Part of me wanted to go back to her, and part of me didn't.

RESPONSIBILITIES

It wasn't all play. One morning Stacy showed Ron and me how to clean the house. She told us she'd had many responsibilities growing up and had to take care of her younger siblings, then added that her family never had much money. "We lived on peanut butter." Every Saturday after that, while Walter was at the bank, she wrote a chore list. We had to clean the bathroom, wipe the walls, dust and sweep. While we cleaned, Pat entertained himself in his room and Stacy would be in her room as well, coming out for moments at a time to make comments like "You missed some marks on that wall" or "The table's still dirty." Then we'd have to wipe them again, which was no big deal. Like my mother, I actually enjoyed cleaning, and this responsibility was like playing house, practice for becoming a grown-up.

We made our own breakfast too, always making sure to clean up to avoid Stacy's wrath. "You left a mess this morning!" And we made our own lunches, which I made sure to do because I didn't want to go hungry. Like Mom, Walter and Stacy believed in eating healthy and were careful with their budget. And Stacy made sure we weren't wasteful. She showed us where to find the stuff for our lunches in the fridge, which was way bigger than the one at Mom's and so full that there were too many items to count: trays of vegetables and fruit, creamy not powdered milk, bottles of sauces and dressings and an array of cheeses and meats. "On your sandwich you can have one slice of cheese and one slice of meat, no more. If you want, you can have two cookies and an apple." I was excited about the store-bought cookies. Dad's oatmeal chocolate chip! Mom had never bought cookies. She said they were a luxury we didn't need.

Practically every evening at mealtime Walter would say, "Well, Mom, what's for dinner? It sure smells good! How was everyone's day?"

I wondered if he called Stacy "Mom" because none of us kids did—not even Pat, who copied us—and he felt that someone should. It wasn't until I became a parent myself that I realized Walter had used the title as a term of endearment. That said, my aunt and uncle didn't seem to mind being addressed by their given names.

While we ate meals like tuna casserole or beans and wieners, I'd usually talk about school. "My teacher's really nice. She reads to us every day!" Miss McMynn was always patient and kind, even to the students who found the lessons hard. She would kneel by their desks, level with them, and always talk softly. "I had so much fun on the maypole at recess," I said, "I have blisters on my fingers!"

Ron would talk about school too. "There's a boy in my class named Jason. He's from England and he can play soccer with a tennis ball. He's amazing!"

"Wow, he sounds pretty good," Walter would say.

We'd all nod in agreement and Stacy would smile, then talk about her busy workday and the latest crisis she'd dealt with. Little Pat would usually have his cheeks stuffed with food, but he liked to be part of the conversation too. He was still at the "why" stage. Why do people get blisters? Why is the sky blue?

When the food was gone, which didn't take long with a family of five, Stacy would quickly jump up from the table and tell Ron and me to wipe up, then she and Walter would relax on the couch, chatting or watching television while sipping spirits. I remember being taken aback by their drinking because Mom never drank alcohol. I realize now that she knew it could react negatively with her medication. Here, at my aunt and uncle's home, there was always a box of wine and a six-pack in the fridge.

Occasionally, when Walter worked late, Stacy would be joined for a glass of wine by Dawn, who lived down the street, while I went to Dawn's house to keep watch over her little boy, a blond toddler. Even though I wasn't paid, I didn't mind, as he was easy to watch because he was always sleeping. At home in the evenings, after tidying the kitchen, I usually preferred to read in my room, but at Dawn's I had the television to myself so I could watch whatever I liked. The only other time I liked watching shows were the nights when Walter and Stacy went out and Stacy's brother, Mike, came by with pizza. With his dreamy Bee Gees looks, I always put down my book to sit by him and join the boys in cheering for the Vancouver Canucks on CBC.

—⚬⚬⚬—

Later that fall Walter and Stacy took us skiing. They'd bought used equipment at a downtown ski swap, and one cool, clear morning we drove up Mount Seymour. After showing us how to don our equipment, Walter gave us a few quick lessons while Stacy went up the chairlift. "Yeah, that's right. Use your poles to push off, then tuck them behind you and bend at the knees to glide down the hill." We fell a couple of times, but he was encouraging. "Try again. You'll get it." After a few times up and down the bunny hill, he said, "Looks like you guys are doing pretty good, so I'm going to ski with Stacy for a while, and I'll come back to check on you later. Stay together."

"Okay. See you later," we called.

After quite some time with no sign of them returning, we kids were getting pretty good and wanted to try something more challenging. "Why don't we try a bigger hill?" Ron suggested. "Uncle Walter said to stay together, but he didn't say we had to stay here. Follow me," he said and headed for the rope tow. For a few minutes we stood watching as skiers were towed up the mountain. Then, with Pat in the middle, we grabbed on to the rope tow and held on tight. Once we reached the top, Ron went down first, then Pat and finally me.

I pushed off with my poles and bent my knees as Walter had shown us, but the hill was steep and I flew down like lightning, the wind stinging my cheeks. It was all I could do to stay vertical and not hit anybody with skiers weaving in and out in front of me. Uncle Walter hadn't said anything about skiing like that. "Look out!" I yelled as I raced down the hill and skiers shook their poles at me. I crashed at the bottom and lay there, my knee stinging with pain.

"Are you okay?" asked Ron, who'd come up beside me with a bewildered Pat. "Wow, were you ever fast! Can you get up?"

I was able to stand, but my knee ached. Before long a member of the ski patrol came by. "Looks like you may have twisted your knee," he said. "Let's get your gear off. Does it hurt to walk? It looks pretty sore. Are your parents around? What are their names?" Because I could barely walk and was close to tears with pain, Ron told him where he thought Walter and Stacy had gone.

"Your parents should be by shortly," the man said after using his radio. I didn't bother to tell him they weren't my parents. "Here, let's get you into the cabin."

While Ron and Pat returned to the bunny hill, the fellow from the ski patrol helped me hobble to a wooden table where skiers were gathered around mugs of warm drinks. Stacy showed up a few minutes later. "Thanks for watching her," she said graciously, seemingly worried as he filled her in on my injury before returning to his post. After he was out of sight, she turned on me. "Oh, great!" she said, exasperated, her expression turning to a scowl. "I'm going to do another couple of runs, then I guess I'll have to round up the others and we'll have to go home," she said, shaking her head. I looked at her apologetically, fighting back tears of guilt mixed with pain.

After sitting in the cabin alone with ice on my knee for a while, I was joined by the rest of the family, and what was supposed to be a fun family outing was over, all because of me.

⸺

One afternoon just a few weeks later, I came out of school and found that Pat and Ron weren't at our usual meeting spot by the front entrance. We'd been walking to and from school together for months now and hanging out with the neighbourhood kids after school until five o'clock. That afternoon as I stood there wondering where they were, I heard a commotion in "the pit," a wooded area across the street where all the school fights took place. Because it was off the school grounds, teachers couldn't do anything about it. I wandered over to see what was happening and heard a crowd chanting, "Fight, fight!" I pushed through and was shocked to see Ron in the clearing with another boy, Eli, who was at least a head taller. Both had their fists up. I spotted Pat then near the front of the gathering, all wrapped up in the excitement. I didn't want to see Ron get pummelled, so I slipped to the back of the crowd but stayed around because I figured my brother would need help after it was over.

After a few minutes of commotion and jeering shouts, I heard the crowd yelling, "Hit him again! Hit him again!" It took all my courage to move to a place where I could see what was happening. Ron was on top of Eli, who was lying on his back in the dirt, crying, with blood pouring down his face. My brother had beaten him! The crowd was calling for Ron to "finish him off," but Ron wasn't like that. Getting up, he wove his way through the crowd to where I was standing, Pat following behind, punching the air in mimicry.

"Did you see that, Phyllis? Did you see it?" Ron said, bouncing up and down. "Walter told me I needed to stand up to him, and I did! I think I broke his nose!"

"You sure showed him!" Pat said, bouncing up and down too.

Not wanting to admit that I hadn't seen the skirmish, I didn't say anything. Besides, I was so surprised that Ron hadn't been beaten to a pulp that I was speechless. Apparently Eli had been bullying Ron for quite a while, and Ron had finally had enough. I see it now as a release of pent-up anger, a blow for every bully he'd had to put up with the previous couple of years, Eli being the breaking point. From that day on, I'm pretty sure my big brother walked with extra pride in his step.

ACCEPTING THE CIRCUMSTANCES

Looking back, I think our mother was like the women from developing countries I'd read about in historical novels who give up their children so they have a chance at a better life. However, Mom refused to accept the decision until her last meeting with a psychiatrist whom I later realized Ron and I had seen earlier for a one-time visit. I vaguely recall that he had dark, curly hair, kind eyes and a certain warmth about him. He assured Mom that Ron and I were open, empathetic children owing to her love and care, but that we were now in a stage of life when we required "some constancy and support to acquire social, intellectual and vocational skills" and that this was "quite readily available" to us in Walter and Stacy's home. As far as I can tell, this doctor treated our mother with more respect than our social worker and her colleagues did, which makes sense as he had years of mental health training and experience with patients.

In the end Mom apparently decided he was right. As a single parent with no help from our father, she had a hard time taking care of her own affairs, let alone ours, and she felt guilty about the times she'd been mean "when she was not herself," according to a report from the psychiatrist. She felt it was important that we stay together and still be in the family, rather than be put up for adoption by strangers where she could not have regular access to us. With all parties in agreement, including our estranged father—who, I wasn't surprised to discover, did not have the means to care for us and was living in a cheap hotel—Walter and Stacy became our permanent foster parents. Our file was to be tracked every six months. Since our aunt and uncle also had financial concerns and couldn't afford to adopt us, they would receive government funding, which for now was set at about $500 a month.

I felt nauseous when I read the last sentence of the psychiatrist's report. He had written that Ron and I had "a very good chance to grow into fully feeling, normal beings and that in itself could give a great deal of support in the future to Carolyn." But Ron and I were kept in the dark about these expectations. How could we be expected to support her? Had all the adults around us assumed that we understood our mother's behaviour? Were they trying to protect us? Or was my mother's diagnosis of paranoid schizophrenia so misunderstood and so taboo at that time that not one person could take a few moments to explain to us why our lives had been turned upside down?

—∞—

I was about nine and a half when it became clear to me that Ron and I would never live with Mom again. "This is where your mom lives now," Stacy said one cool, cloudy day as she parked her Honda Civic in front of a building in New Westminster. Ron and I walked with her to the front door, where she punched in some numbers. Seconds later Mom came out. Without even saying hello to Mom, Stacy announced she would pick us up in a couple of hours. Mom thanked her, avoiding eye contact.

Upon entering her apartment, I realized her place was way too small for the three of us, and I felt strange being in *her* home rather than *our* home. Ron and my mother must have felt the same because for a few moments we all stood silent and motionless, as if taking in the permanency of the situation. Mom had fit all her belongings and furniture into one room, using the couch as a divider to separate the kitchen from the living area. In the far corner was the free-standing television beside a large window that spanned nearly the width of the room. Under the window stood her dark wooden dresser, and beside that was the double bed we used to share. Granny's old vanity stood opposite by the television.

"Well, what do you think?" Mom asked, breaking the silence.

"It's nice, Mom," Ron and I politely agreed.

"I made some tomato soup and grilled cheese sandwiches for lunch," Mom said as she walked into the tiny kitchen to scoop soup into bowls. "How are Walter and Stacy treating you?"

We had to squeeze ourselves in between the couch and the kitchen table to sit down. We told her they treated us fine and then talked about school and the new friends we'd made.

"That's good," Mom replied calmly, back to her old self.

Over the next couple of months we would visit her for a couple of hours every other weekend. When each visit came to an end, I had a lump in my throat and my eyes would start to swim, but eventually I accepted the way things were.

One afternoon at Mom's apartment, I remember searching through copies of *Reader's Digest* for interesting recipes while Ron designed mazes.

"What about this one, Mom?" I asked.

"That looks good," she answered as she sat at the table smoking. Then I wrote the instructions down in my crooked handwriting in a little book framed in blue and titled *Recipes*. I don't remember if Mom ever made any of the recipes I copied that day, but it was nice to spend time with her. Afterwards we tried to crack one of Ron's tricky mazes, but I didn't have the patience to deal with the tangled mass of lines.

"You try," I said to Mom.

"I give up," she said, waving her hands in defeat.

Ron grabbed the notepad. "It's easy! Look! You just go down this way, turn here, turn to the left …"

On warm days we'd either toss a Frisbee or have a picnic at the nearby park, where we had a view of the Pattullo Bridge spanning the Fraser River. The park's large maples provided shade where we'd enjoy the sandwiches and cups of Kool-Aid Mom put out on a tray. Other times we'd walk to Queen's Park. As we headed up the incline, I'd be taken by the size of the houses—nines and tens and some even off my scale—and I would stop to admire them as I'd done at Deer Lake, these proud homes standing as tall as kings on a castle with their fancy deck furniture and shiny barbecues perched on porches the size of my mother's whole apartment.

With Mom doing so well, Pat even came with us on occasion. I remember that one time we wandered down Columbia Street and Mom stopped to get a coffee, which she drank as we sat on the curb in front of the café. Another time we met her new boyfriend, Roger, a quiet man who walked with a limp. He pulled his dark, curly hair back and wore it in a ponytail. As when she had met our father, Mom met him at a bus stop. "He asked me for a cigarette," Mom told us as we sat at the table enjoying bologna sandwiches one afternoon. "Next thing I knew, I invited him for coffee."

Later Roger told me that at nineteen he had been in a motorcycle crash, and not long after that he had developed depression. "I had my whole life ahead of me and it was taken away just like that," he said, snapping his fingers. "The driver of the truck walked away scot-free, not even a scratch. Do you think he's suffering at all?"

I didn't really know how I felt about Roger at first, but when I told Walter about him, he said, "Well, he's probably good for your mother. She needs a friend, and it gives her something to do and someone to care for." I figured he was right. Mom could use the company. Besides, Roger had a gentle manner, and as far as I could tell, he didn't rile her up as Uncle Jack and Gilbert had.

YEAR OF THE CHILD

I was reading a Nancy Drew novel in my bedroom one afternoon when Walter handed me a rectangular package to open. "This is for you," he said, continuing down the hall to change out of the suit he wore for work. Curious, I removed the yellowy-brown paper, and inside was a book with the title *Watch Me Grow* in shiny gold letters with an acorn below. On the first page was an inscription:

> This book has been designed for you as a special gift in the Year of the Child and Family in British Columbia. May this book help you to record your experiences, feelings and events that are important to you in your life.
> With all best wishes.
> Sincerely,
> Deputy Premier,
> Minister of Human Resources

Each page had its own subtitle with lines to write on and a large envelope to store keepsakes and pictures: My Name, My Health Record, My Family, My Firsts, My First Year, My Second Year, My Third Year and so on. When Walter popped in to see what was in the package, I showed him the page entitled My Family Tree, and he offered, "Your father's name is Ray. He lived in the low-income complex down the street from us in Ottawa. He couldn't have had an easy life. His mother was a widow with twelve kids. I don't recall their names, but they were like a gang. If you messed with one, you messed with them all."

"Are my freckles from my father?" I had a smattering of freckles across my nose, and Mom didn't have any.

"Must be. He was a redhead," he replied.

After he left the room, I thought about Walter's words and felt compassion for the father I couldn't remember. I wrote his name, lingering a few moments, repeating it. *Ray.* I liked it. Then I filled in what I could of my mother's side of the family tree, the schools I'd attended, my teachers and the friends who had come and gone from my life, leaving the remaining pages and keepsake envelopes empty. Then I stored this special book in my closet, making a mental note to update it every so often, which I now see was an attempt to capture my sense of identity. Through the changing seasons for the rest of my childhood, I'd turn another page and fill it with as many mementoes, names of relatives and special people as I could. And sometimes I'd stand in front of the bathroom mirror and stare at my freckles, the spots I'd inherited from my father, who, like me, had lost his father.

—∞—

In the summer of 1979, when I was nearly ten, we went camping again, this time near McBride in eastern BC. After all the canoe lessons we'd taken, Walter and Stacy must have figured we had the skills to face the challenge of paddling the mighty Fraser River, but it didn't help that rain poured the entire time. It would have been difficult enough navigating the rapids in dry weather, let alone in rain slickers when we were all wet and cold.

We woke each morning in our damp tent, shivering as we donned our rain gear. Stacy navigated from the stern in one canoe while eleven-year-old Ron manned the bow. In the other, Walter navigated from the stern, while I manned the bow. Pat and Blackie sat on the floor between us, and I kept wishing I could join them there rather than fight the current and follow Walter's continuous commands. "Backpaddle! Now front! J-stroke! Quick! There's a tree leaning over the river ahead!" At one point Blackie was so scared that he jumped out of the canoe into the frigid waters to seek refuge on shore, and Walter had to coax him back in. "Come on, boy! It's okay! That's right!"

I can't say whether it was the rain that proved too much or the strength of the current, but I was very happy when Walter and Stacy cut our journey short, and when we stashed the canoes in the bush and took refuge in a motel, I quietly cheered.

—∞—

Shortly after my tenth birthday, Stacy set the foundation of our future relationship quite firmly. We were at her parents' place, acreage they had recently bought in a rural area on the city's outskirts. I hadn't seen her parents since the previous summer when we kids had gorged on the fruit from the cherry trees in their suburban backyard while the adults talked inside. (We paid for our greed later and spent the evening running to the bathroom!) On this day, too, we spent most of our time atop a cherry tree, enjoying the fruit's juicy sweetness until our fingers and tongues were stained pink.

Although Stacy's father, Grandpa Joe, walked with a limp similar to Roger's—an injury from an accident he'd had in his younger days—it didn't slow him down. He was a tall, sturdy man who held his head high and spoke in a low, gentle tone. As I sat in the cherry tree, I could hear him talking as he showed Uncle Walter his beehives in the meadow, though I couldn't hear his actual words. "He's one of the best beekeepers in the Lower Mainland," Uncle Walter had told us. "He never gets stung because he just moves slowly and calmly, and those bees don't even know he's there." When he wasn't beekeeping, Grandpa Joe drove a disposal truck for the City of Burnaby.

Stacy's mother was a homemaker who liked the drink. Family rumour had it that she hid liquor around the house, though there was no hiding liquor on this night. After a hearty stew followed by tart rhubarb from the garden that we dipped in sugar, we kids were sent to our sleeping bags in the room beside the lounge area, where the adults sat clutching beer mugs and wineglasses. Stacy's sister, Georgina, who was the spitting image of Stacy, only blond, had joined the party by then too.

I fell asleep quickly but was awakened by the sound of women's laughter. Then I heard Georgina's high-pitched voice saying, "So what's it like having two more children in the house?"

"It's great," Stacy replied. "They clean the house. They do the dishes. It's like having two little maids."

I didn't hear anything else after that. My mind was racing. I wasn't mature enough to think about how hard it must be for my aunt to have extra children in her home or all the changes she had to cope with. All I could think about were all the thankless chores we did. Her hurtful words left me wondering whether she truly cared for us at all.

Days later, when Walter and Stacy were out, Ron and I were doing the dishes, and I told him what I'd heard. "Stacy doesn't love us, Ron. She doesn't care about us at all. We're just workers to her."

"She really said that?"

"Yep. I heard it with my own ears. It's not really surprising. We do all the cleaning every Saturday. She doesn't even help!" I said, placing dishes in the cupboard. "She never even hugs us or holds our hands. When was the last time she asked about our day? Never! You know why? Because she doesn't care. All she cares about is whether we've done our chores."

"Yeah, I guess."

I went into mimic mode then, imitating her demanding voice: "Phyllis, have you made your bed? It's time to do the dishes!"

And there I was, mimicking her, when I turned around to see her standing in the living room, listening. Uncle Walter was there too. With all the clattering of the dishes, we hadn't heard them come in. I scanned their faces, wondering how much they'd heard. By their stern looks, I could tell they'd heard enough that I was in deep trouble.

Uncle Walter was first to speak. "Ron, Phyllis, when you're done, go to your rooms." We obeyed silently, not knowing what would happen next, though I knew it wouldn't be good. While Mom had a wooden spoon that she never used, Uncle Walter had a paddle about as long as his arm that looked as if it had been whittled by hand. He entered my room carrying it, sat beside me on the bed and placed the paddle across his lap. I couldn't take my eyes off it as it lay there threatening me.

"You can't speak about your aunt Stacy that way," he said. "It's not respectful. I don't want you to ever talk about her like that again. I can't believe you would say those things, especially after all we've done for you." I nodded in mute agreement, but I was thinking that what she'd said wasn't exactly respectful either, and he didn't bother to ask my side of the story. "You need to be taught a lesson. Bend over." As I lay across his lap, he hit my behind three times, so hard that I wet my pants just enough to leave a small, wet circle on his jeans. "That should give you something to think about. There will be no dinner for you tonight."

While I lay crying and feeling sorry for myself, I decided I would tell Mom what Stacy had said, as her words had hurt more than Walter's paddle. I don't really know what I expected to come of my decision, but I had to tell someone about the situation that I viewed as unfair. I knew Mom would hear me out. After all, she had defended me when I had told her about Uncle Jack.

On our next visit she listened intently, nodding every once in a while. "Hmm, is that right?" she'd say. She wasn't much of a talker, but she was a good listener. I didn't tell her about the paddle. I had a soft spot for my uncle's fatherly grin. Sure enough, after our visit, Mom asked Stacy if they could talk for a few minutes, and Stacy agreed hesitantly. "You guys wait in the car."

Mom must have told Stacy off good because minutes later my aunt sat in the driver's seat, slammed the door, turned around to the back seat and, before I had a chance to think or say anything, slapped me hard across the face. *Whack!* My head was forced to one side by the blow, my cheek stinging with pain. Ron looked on with fear and surprise.

"Don't you ever talk to your mother about me like that again!" she raged, before turning her attention back to the car.

At that moment I felt a change, an indescribable feeling deep within my soul. It didn't matter how I felt. It didn't matter what I said. I had no control. Not even Mom could help.

Part Three

FROM CARS TO TRUCKS

I wonder what Mom thought when in the late winter of 1981 our blended family moved to the Cariboo, a way of life that was completely different and miles away from the city. I wasn't at all fazed by the relocation, as I don't think I understood the ramifications. I was just going through the motions in a daze, resigned to my fate. I don't remember saying goodbye to Mom or worrying that I'd miss her. I'd grown used to not living with her, and with visits reduced to "special occasions" since she and Stacy had their talk, I hardly saw her anymore. Months had gone by since I complained, "I wish I still lived with Mom. She never made me clean the bathroom!"

To prepare for the move, Walter and Stacy had sold their rancher months earlier and rented a duplex in Delta, and Walter spent weeks perusing home builders' magazines. I remember him showing me some of the odd-looking houses in them. Some were circular domes, and I'd wondered how furniture could be found for such places, while others were built into the side of a hill. I had commented, "That's just like the dugout the Ingallses in the *Little House on the Prairie* books lived in. Their cow fell through the roof."

"Really?" Walter said, laughing.

Usually when I'd arrived at another new school, it had taken me a long time to fit in. This time, when I heard a couple of boys talking about a Vancouver Canucks game, I impressed them when I piped up with "Oh yeah, Richard Brodeur made a great save."

"You saw the game?" one boy asked. Watching the Canucks had become a family pastime. I knew the name and jersey number of every player. From that day on, boys in the class would randomly ask questions like "What number is Darcy Rota?" or "Who scored the winning goal last night?" I always knew the answer. Even the girls were impressed. And just like that, I was accepted.

I remember that my teacher at the school in Delta, Mrs. Carson,

gave me a parting card. At lunch break I was mingling with the classmates I'd never really get to know when she called me to her desk
to hand me an envelope. "Goodbye and good luck," she said. I think
I muttered, "Thanks," surprised by the gesture. I figured she couldn't
have thought too highly of me as my report cards were far from great.
While I was a whiz at hockey stats, I wasn't even close to the top of
my class anymore, though I made sure to complete my assignments so
I wouldn't fail.

Ron had his struggles too. Sometime before leaving the city, he
threatened to run away. At the time I'd looked to Walter, relaxing on
the couch, and he read the worry on my face. "He'll be fine." He was
right. Ron was home by nightfall, but our aunt and uncle were apparently concerned. With my slipping grades, they had told our new social
worker, whose face I can't recall, that I was "a little slow," and with Ron
failing grade seven, they filled out paperwork demonstrating that we
were "needy" and required "extra supervision." As a result, for months
they had been receiving special rates to take care of us, up from $500 to
$800 monthly, a tidy sum back then.

While I believe that Walter and Stacy underestimated the amount
of time and effort they would need to achieve their dream of building
a log house and living off the land, they had taken out a mortgage in
order to buy acreage thirty miles southeast of the small Cariboo town
where Walter found work at one of the local banks. However, before
moving north, they traded in both of their cars for a pickup. We left
town while the people in the other houses on the street were still sleeping, including my friend Jody, who lived across the street. After school
each day, while Ron and Pat played street hockey or nicky nicky nine
doors, I had hung out with her, usually skipping rope or playing hop-
scotch until Walter and Stacy returned from work at five o'clock. When
I'd said goodbye the evening before we left and told her that I'd miss
her, she had stood in the middle of the road with a forlorn look, watching me quietly as I walked away. I'd turned back every few moments
to wave goodbye, and the sad expression on her face had made me feel
guilty for leaving. I can still picture her freckled face and bouncy hair, a
frozen snapshot in my memory.

Walter said we had to leave early to "beat the traffic," which could
have been partly true, but now that I think of it, it was more likely

because he didn't want anyone to see us depart. That morning, as the sun was dawning and black clouds were gathering in the distance, Stacy and Pat climbed onto the bench seat of the truck's cab, but I couldn't help but notice that there wasn't room there for Ron and me. It wasn't a problem, though. Uncle Walter had already thought of that and had his arms full of quilts.

"Hey, guys," he said, "you get to travel in the back. Look at all the room you have! Climb in and lie down. I'll help you get comfortable."

Part of me thought it was odd to be travelling in the metal box that was lined with a sheet of plywood, but I trusted that Uncle Walter would keep us safe as by now he was like a father to us. We climbed up and lay on top of one of the thick floral comforters he'd spread out. Then he covered us with another comforter and tucked it in around us.

"How's that?" he asked. "You comfortable?"

"Yep, we're good," we answered.

If Blackie had been around, he would have likely been in the back of the truck too, but several months earlier he'd disappeared from Stacy's parents' place, where he was being looked after temporarily. While we kids were playing in the meadow one day, we'd asked Walter, "Where's Blackie?"

"Blackie? He's long gone. Went missing just days after we dropped him off. He was probably chasing cattle or chickens and got shot by a farmer. That dog had a wild streak. He never stayed put," he said matter-of-factly, as if Blackie hadn't been the beloved family pet. We were devastated.

"All right then," Walter now said cheerfully. "Just remember to keep your heads down under the quilts, okay? You'll be warmer that way. You can even have a nap if you want."

That's exactly what we did. Having awoken earlier than usual, we quickly fell asleep under the blankets while Walter, Stacy and Pat travelled comfortably in the warm cab. Nobody could tell that there were two children travelling like stowaways in the back of a pickup. We could have been luggage or tools, the quilts vibrating over us in the wind, heading north on Highway 1. I remember waking a couple of hours later and propping myself up to get a view of the spectacular, jagged, amber-and-grey-hued cliffs sprinkled with evergreen trees and a frosting of snow on their peaks. At the bottom of the canyon, below the highway's cliff edge, I could see the Fraser River bubbling with white spray and foam.

While I stared in awe, I heard Stacy's voice loaded with annoyance. She had opened the sliding rear window of the cab. "Keep your head down, Phyllis!" she yelled. "Put it down under the covers!" I slipped down just enough to still see the sights, but Aunt Stacy continued yelling, "Keep your head down, Phyllis!"

By this time Ron was awake too, and since this section of the highway had many twists and turns, we made a game of rolling from side to side under the covers as our bodies moved with the momentum. "Whoa!" we said, laughing as our bodies swayed to one side as we turned a corner and rolled into each other. "Whoa!" we exclaimed again as our bodies swayed back the other way. And when the vehicle plunged into the dimly lit tunnels of the Fraser Canyon, we made a game of holding our breath until daylight appeared again. At one point along the way it started to rain, but fortunately the quilts kept us dry and warm. A few hours later, having reached our destination, Walter pulled off the highway, and I meekly peeped my head out from under the covers in case Aunt Stacy yelled at me again.

When Walter cut the engine, I sat up and was shocked at the sight. Our home-to-be was a far cry from the suburban homes we'd left behind. The first of the two rented homes we would settle in while Walter and Stacy's dreams were brought to fruition was nothing more than a decrepit wooden shack surrounded by a grove of pine trees. With spring breakup, the winter frost had begun melting out of the ground, creating a yard of oozing mud. A large wooden shed that would later become Walter's workshop stood opposite the house, and beside that was a tiny weathered cottage they would rent to a couple of city friends who would pretty much keep to themselves.

I'd rate the building that was to become our home as a three. Decades earlier it might have been bright and fresh looking, but it was well past its prime. However, I soon discovered that it wasn't too different from most of the other homes along the highway, weathered shacks just like our home, threes and fours, while others were even worse, nothing more than twos, shoddy plywood shanties with smoke billowing from tin chimneys. But there were also a few quaint cabins and some standard modern houses, all ranging between seven and eight, and every so often a majestic log home, a nine or ten.

On entering the decrepit building we were to call home, I saw that the wooden step was rickety, the old timber door creaked, the linoleum floor of the kitchen was yellowed with age and the countertops were covered in brownish-yellow stains. Most of the rooms had wood panelling, while what seemed to have been the original building before other rooms were added had aged log walls with cracks between them where daylight shone through. In the days that followed, Walter would go through at least four tubes of caulking to fill in the holes.

I could tell that Ron and Pat were feeling the same dismay I was, and Walter, noticing our faces, did his best to make light of the situation. "Hey, it's not so bad," he said. "And the price couldn't be better. It's free!"

"It'll be fine," Stacy agreed, "and it'll look better once we're settled." She would spend weeks cleaning and organizing, trying to make the place look civilized.

"Walter, where's the bathroom?" I asked on that first day, needing to go after all the travelling.

"There's an outhouse out back," he said. Seeing my look of disgust, he added, "It'll be like camping! And it's just temporary. It won't be long before we have a beautiful log home and a farm of our own, won't we, honey?" he said, turning to Stacy, who nodded and grinned. He added, "It'll be just like the farm I remember as a boy in Manitoba." Later he hung a black and white photo in the hall, a picture of himself as a boy of about twelve with his fresh-faced young father and an uncle I'd never met leaning on an antique tractor. They were all wearing work clothes—light-coloured shirts, worn leather shoes and trousers held up by suspenders—and standing in a meadow, which Walter said was part of his grandparents' farm, where my mother was born.

Sure enough, at the end of a muddy path on the northwest side of the house was a shed-roofed outhouse made of aged, blackened plywood. We'd keep a flashlight by the kitchen door for late-night callings. One morning, shortly after we'd settled, I wandered into the kitchen and was assaulted by a smell so strong I almost gagged.

"Pat! Get in here," Uncle Walter yelled angrily from the mud room after he discovered where the pungent smell was coming from. Young

Pat, scared of the dark, shadowy night, had relieved himself in an empty pop bottle.

As time went on, it was hard to tell which was worse: the ice-cold plastic toilet seat in winter or the awful smell and incessant mosquitoes when the weather turned warm. But living in this dump had its advantages. There was no bathroom to clean and no gleaming walls to wipe. But, besides dish duty, Ron and I now had a different set of chores. Bathing was a chore in itself. Every Sunday we would all bathe in the kitchen by the warmth of the wood stove, and it became my job to prepare the aluminum tub stored behind the couch. With no running hot water, I would fill the tub with two or three inches of water I'd heated on the propane stove. I hated lighting that darn stove, having never forgotten how devastating fire could be. Its flame would whoosh up, scaring me, and I'd quickly snatch the match away, shaking it out at the same time a burning sensation crept up my arm.

To allow privacy, the rest of the family would either retire to the family room or to their bedrooms. We took turns bathing by age, youngest first, and the water would be grey and murky by the time it was Ron's turn. (Walter and Stacy must have bathed later while we were in bed because I don't remember them bathing, though I'm sure they did.) One Sunday evening while Pat was bathing, I was at the sink wiping dishes with my back to the tub to allow him privacy when I was interrupted by the sound of his yelps. "Ow, ow!" When I turned to see what all the yelling was about, I had to stifle my laughter as he was jumping around in his birthday suit, clutching his pained bottom, which he'd been warming by the wood stove.

Stacy came running, glass of wine in hand. "What's wrong? Is everything okay?" She wasn't pleased that her time on the sofa with Walter had been interrupted.

"I burned my butt! I burned my butt!" Pat yelled, hopping around.

"Is that all? Let me see. You're fine! Don't get so close to the stove next time."

Stacy loved spending time with Walter. If we kids played board games with him in the evenings, she'd holler, "When are you coming to bed?" We'd exchange anxious looks, worried he wouldn't finish our game.

"I'll be there after we're done," he'd call back. "Won't be too long."

I felt sorry for him at times. He was like the rope in a tug-of-war.

Stacy was pulling him in one direction and we youngsters were pulling him in the other.

———

As wood heat was all we had, and we needed at least six cords of wood a year, on weekends Walter would use his chainsaw to slice up the fallen trees he found along the deserted back roads, while the family donned work gloves and loaded it into the bed of the truck. Walter also taught Ron, who was now thirteen, to use an axe, a sledgehammer and a wedge to chop up the rounds so they'd fit into the stove. Ron would hold his head high, swinging the axe while sweat poured down his face. I could tell he was proud of all the firewood he chopped, the power he had developed and the muscles he was honing. Stacking the wood left me toned too, and when no chips were flying, Pat got exercise as well, picking up the small pieces to use for kindling. He'd puff out his chest while chopping thin rounds with a small axe, acting older than his eight years and pretending to be like Ron.

As in the city, the three of us saw ourselves off to school, but on cool days, before catching the yellow bus, Ron and I had to light the fire first. Now that I was older, he taught me the fire-starting skills Walter had taught him along with the tips he'd learned at Scouts. "You can make a teepee or a log cabin with the kindling," he explained patiently. I opted for the teepee version, which was quicker, and as Walter stood by, now it was my turn to beam when the wood caught fire. We also had to tend to the few black Angus cows kept within a snake-fenced enclosure up a slight hill by the old barn. They were being fattened up for the freezer. We'd climb the barn ladder and drop the hay bales down from the loft. Ron could lift the twine-wrapped bales easily; they were too heavy for me, but I'd push or slide them around, appreciating the explosion patterns the hay created when the bales hit the ground and the cows wandered over to eat.

You'd think that, being siblings, we would have bickered about our duties, but we never did. After all we'd been through, we were closer now than ever. I think deep down we recognized that we were all each other had, so we shared our tasks and worked together. We'd fill ten-gallon buckets with water from the outdoor tap, then haul them up the path to the bathtub trough. I quickly learned to fill the buckets halfway, not only to lighten the load but also because I didn't want the water to slosh all over me as I walked. Come winter, when the water had frozen, we'd trudge up the snowy path Ron and Walter had shovelled, carrying kettles of boiled water to melt the ice.

As much as those cows seemed lazy, at times they jumped the fence and wandered off to visit Javier, our neighbour to the south. "Darn those cows!" Walter would say, then he'd yell for Ron.

"Coming!" Ron would arrive in the kitchen, all broad shoulders and head held high, to put on his mac and workboots. They'd be gone a long time, rounding up the cows and tending the fence so the animals would stay put. By the time they were home again, they had spent hours bonding man to man, though before long Javier would be on the phone again. "A couple of your cows are over here again!"

Javier's son, Marc, who was my age, walked with a swagger and a lopsided smile, and as soon as we met, we took a liking to each other, making eyes on the school bus. As our stop was last, after all the other kids were off the bus, sometimes he'd come to sit with me and hold my hand while we exchanged shy smiles. Then at a neighbourhood pig roast his family hosted later that spring, he found me hiding in the barn during a game of kick the can, and we had just enough time to share a nervous kiss before other kids came by to hide. That same night, while the adults were busy enjoying drinks, Marc and Ron snuck off with cans of beer. When Ron didn't feel too well the next day, Stacy didn't find their antics funny, but Walter only chuckled. "It's part of growing up!" he said.

A few days later when we were on the school bus, Marc presented me with a silver ring, but our young love didn't last. It wasn't long before I gave it back because he never talked to me at school, as though he was embarrassed to be with me. However, his friendship with Ron lasted for many years.

⸺

In mid-spring Walter bought a used four-by-four Jimmy, a truck that could fit all of us and safely navigate the back roads, and we ventured out to visit the acreage Walter and Stacy had purchased. After heading south a few miles, we turned east and drove for a couple of hours on a maze of gravel roads with Stacy anxiously telling Walter to slow down.

Finally we crossed the single-lane bridge over the Silver River and, turning onto a narrow dirt driveway, we arrived at a well-built cabin, a seven, standing on the edge of a meadow with pine trees out back. It came complete with rustic furniture, dishes and a small loft where we kids were to sleep.

The next morning, while Walter and Stacy set up house, we kids were exploring the meadow when a patchwork cat wandered over to visit.

"What's a cat doing in the middle of nowhere?" I asked Walter.

"Maybe she was left here by the previous owners," he said.

"Can we keep her?" we begged.

"She looks well fed," Stacy replied.

"She seems to be doing fine on her own," Walter added, as the cat wandered into the large metal shed nearby.

When it was time to leave, we asked again if we could take the cat home and were disappointed when Walter answered, "She knows how to survive. She's been here this long."

The thing with survival is that trying to stay alive in the middle of a forest full of predators is tricky. A few weeks later when we returned and ran to the shed to find her, we noticed paw prints in the oozing mud. "Look, Walter! What are these?" we asked, pointing.

"Well, this doesn't look good," he said, bending low to the ground. "There's been a chase. These are cat prints and these bigger ones that look like dog prints are coyote." That was our first of many lessons in animal tracking. Later he'd teach us to identify the animal tracks of deer, moose and bear, as well as their scat. It was particularly important to recognize fresh bear droppings.

"Do you think the cat got away?" we asked hopefully.

"I reckon not," Walter said. "But that's how life is. Survival of the fittest."

For weeks I longed for that dear little cat to wander over again, hoping my uncle was wrong, but unfortunately he was right. His words still echo today.

—∞—

Once the spring thaw was over, the weekends were filled with preparations for Walter and Stacy's dream home on the new property. Pat, in particular, enjoyed the show when big machines cleared the hillside on which the house would stand, giving us a view of the river and the island meadow. After the well was dug and the plumbing was ready, it was time to pour the foundation. I remember sorting stones, the large from the small, so the gravel could be mixed with concrete. While Walter figured out how to operate the mixer, the rest of us sat among the rocks on the hillside, throwing stones that were too large toward the riverbank. "Be careful!" Stacy had told us, wary of our safety. "Watch where you throw. You don't want to hit anyone." Yet within moments I felt a wallop on my forehead, the impact not quite painful enough to draw tears. When I glanced in the direction the stone had come from, expecting it to be one of the boys, I was surprised to discover that it was Stacy who had just ignored her own safety warnings. "Sorry," she said in a way that made it sound as if it were my fault my head had got in the way. To this day, I don't know what hurt more, the stone or her offhand apology.

Once the concrete was mixed and poured into the forms, we kids used waist-high two-by-fours to aerate and level it out. I found the repetitive motion of lifting the piece of wood up and down through the soft grey mass almost therapeutic, much like a child working a piece of clay.

With all the activity going on and the dust being kicked up, Walter trailered in an old bathtub. He placed it by the river, perched it up on rocks, added a rusty stovepipe, filled it with buckets of river water and then built a fire underneath. After lining the bottom of the tub with a flat piece of wood so as not to scald his precious bottom, he climbed into it in his birthday suit with a beer in hand and a smile on his face, pretty chuffed with his invention.

Meanwhile, Walter and Stacy had been telling us for months that they might take in more foster children. "It would be great to have another strong, capable boy, another pair of hands to help out." The lad, about my age, came to the cabin one weekend for a trial run. He failed the audition, as he was much too troubled. He was rude to Walter and Stacy and made fun of Ron, calling him names and putting him down. One evening after we'd settled to burgers, Walter asked him to remove the cap he wore over his ginger hair, and he refused, which didn't fly well. He was sent back, and Walter and Stacy never mentioned the idea of more foster children again.

One unusually hot spring day, we surprised a young family cooling off in the river. As we approached the narrow wooden bridge, we saw they were all naked! The woman stood ankle-deep in the gentle rapids, her long, blond hair hanging over her breasts and her hands on the shoulders of her curly-haired daughter, whom she held in front of her to cover what still needed to be covered. The man, who had long, wavy brown hair, stood holding the youngest daughter in front of what needed to be covered as well.

I was flabbergasted when Walter stopped the vehicle and turned down the radio so he could talk to these nudists. (Whenever we went to the cabin, Stacy liked to rock out in her seat to the beats of Supertramp, the Cars or Meatloaf. Not me. I preferred to sing melodies of peace and harmony to myself, songs I'd learned in school like "I'd Like to Teach the World to Sing" or "This Land Is Your Land.")

"Hi there. Lovely day, isn't it?" Walter said. "Good idea to cool off in the river."

"Yeah," they agreed. "Nice day."

They exchanged pleasantries as if they were old friends before we continued on our way. The next day we drove about twenty minutes to what I now realize was a hippie commune, where this young family lived. About twenty tents were spread out in the meadow beside the river. Adults with long hair and earth-coloured clothes were roaming around: men with ponytails or dreadlocks and women in peasant skirts with long, flowing hair or beaded braids. When I saw some children romping around, all my young self could think about was how these families survived way out in the boonies, particularly in the frosty winter.

While Walter and Stacy chatted with their new friends, Kayla and Joshua, we kids spent the afternoon running around with four girls, happy to have company their age. Their names were so unusual that I've never forgotten them: Ocean, Rose, Sky and Pearl. They all had long, prettily braided hair strung with beads that I admired and was a little envious of. "Our mom did them for us," they said. Since we'd left Mom, nobody did my hair anymore. I was old enough to fancy it up myself by then, but I couldn't be bothered. Later, as we wandered along a trail, I was surprised when the girls told us they didn't even go to school.

I never asked, but part of me wondered if they'd ever been to the city. From the city myself, I was like a celebrity at our local school, so it was easy for me to join in games of tag. My classmates all seemed to have relatives there. "My aunt lives in Surrey" or "I have an uncle who lives in Burnaby," they'd say. Everyone, that is, except David, a classmate who told me that he'd lived in the same house all his life and had never left town, which was really hard to imagine, considering all the places I'd lived.

When I told Walter about David, he said, "That boy's missing so many life experiences. You've got way more life experience than he has. That will serve you well one day." Later I thought about my uncle's words. Living within the same four walls in the same small town for years hadn't made for a broad range of experiences for David. He had never seen a skyscraper, never ridden a city bus. Even so, as an adult I would see that David had what I'd never had as a child: the security of a stable home. He'd never had to deal with the difficult transitions of every move Ron and I had made, like making new friends and leaving old friends behind. By grade six, I was in my fifth school.

Back at our shack of a home, I was stacking wood while Ron fetched a glass of water, taking a break from the rigours of wood chopping, when Walter came out and told me he'd be taking Ron to the hospital in a few days. "We'll be gone about a week. It's nothing serious, but he's wetting the bed again. They apparently have a really good program that can help him."

I looked at him questioningly. Ron was a teenager now. At least Walter and Stacy were more discreet, I thought, than Lady Stranger had been and had kept his whole ordeal quiet. Walter must have read my thoughts. "Well, he's been through some rough times. He's had a harder time than you've had. Your mom's never liked men. Can't really blame her. Whenever she went into hospital, the police, the paramedics, they were all men. She liked me though. I was just a kid when she got sick. Everyone else argued with her and riled her up, but I just listened, so we got along fine."

"Yeah, I guess," I replied, not really comprehending what he was saying. "We've both been through a lot."

"I suppose," he said in agreement, his eyes growing distant. "Yep, I remember those days. Your uncle Jack was a great athlete then. He could swim across the Ottawa River." When he turned to me, his eyes were swimming. "You know, one way to look at it is there's always someone worse off than you. Always remember that." Then he walked slowly back inside.

Taking his words of optimism to heart, I thought there really were people worse off than us. At least we'd never had to live in a tent. I could see that thoughts of his older brother upset Walter, but, at eleven, I didn't have the context to figure out why. Later, with years of life behind me, I'd realize that he'd seen the older brother he'd once admired soar, then plummet.

The day after my brother and Walter departed, I disembarked from the noisy school bus, looking forward to reading in the peace of my bedroom, but when I got there, I saw that my dolls and stuffed animals weren't lovingly lined across my pillow.

I heard Stacy in the hall. "Where are my dolls?" I asked.

Vacuum cleaner in hand, she answered, "Oh, I gave them to Kayla and Joshua." They'd moved into a cabin a few miles to the south of us. I guess they didn't like living in a tent.

"But ..."

"You're too old to play with dolls."

"But ..."

At that point she must have sensed how upset I was because she answered quickly, "It's too late. I can't get them back."

I realize now that in one of her cleaning frenzies, she had simply cleaned out my dolls without thinking how I would feel, but at the time I could tell by her I'm-too-busy-to-care tone of voice that there would be no changing her mind. Fighting back tears, I turned back to my room and lay on my empty bed. I knew that Kayla and Joshua didn't have much money, but Stacy had just given away my only keepsake from my father, my only connection to him, his one gift. Over the years I'd sometimes held that special doll and thought about my father with his freckles and red hair, hoping we'd see each other again one day. Now I'd never hold my Inuit doll again. There was no more Baby Laura either. No more sleeping with any of my beloved dolls so I wouldn't be lonely. I lay on my friendless bed trying not to think about those curly-headed girls holding what was mine.

Then after a few moments I realized I wasn't completely alone. In the bottom corner of the wall near the end of my bed was a little brown spider. I watched the small creature, standing strong and silent in its web, for a few moments before going to sit beside it on the floor. As there was nobody else to talk to, in my head I began talking to the spider. In the magical silence I told the wee critter, whom I named Fred, about my terrible situation. I was like the orphan girl in *Anne of Green Gables* who talked to flowers. I just happened to talk to a spider instead. And for days Fred brought me comfort.

After a dinner of empty conversation without Walter there to pull the family together, and after my chores were done, while Stacy watched television and Pat played in his room, I'd sit and read by the little fellow who helped to ease my pain and take away my feelings of loneliness. Then after school one day, Fred, like my treasured dolls, was gone, but I was okay, as I knew spiders didn't live forever. While I was unaware of it at the time, my coping mechanism had worked. I was over my grief. Although I'd lost my Inuit doll, her everlasting image lives in my memory, where nobody can take away that most valued connection to my father. As for the day Walter and Ron returned home, and every day thereafter, my brother's bed stayed dry and cozy.

⸺

That summer Walter and Stacy arranged for Mom and Roger to come to the cabin for a visit. I was filled with excitement when Walter, Ron and I picked them up at the roadside bus stop on the highway, greeting them with a big hug. When we hit the gravel road, Mom wasn't thrilled with the potholes, but with Stacy not around to insist on abiding by the speed limits, Walter made a game of wildly steering round them and we yelped with laughter. I can still hear Mom's screeching giggles. After polite greetings were exchanged with Stacy and Pat, who were hanging out in the yard, I held the crook of Mom's arm as I'd always done, and while Roger chatted with Walter, Ron and I acted as tour guides as we wandered down the meadow.

"That's the pond where I lost one of my boots. The mud sucked it right off my foot!" Ron exclaimed while she laughed.

"That's the climbing tree," I told her, pointing. "And I can climb almost to the top!"

"That's so high! Careful you don't fall!"

"Don't worry, we're great climbers!"

When we arrived at the clearing where the log house would stand, she and Roger commented on the view. They also commented on the bathtub.

"Want a bath?" Walter said. "Hop in!"

They laughed, refusing his offer.

After the tour Mom helped us kids collect sticks for a hot dog and marshmallow roast, and she and Roger were impressed when Ron whittled them sharp with his jackknife. More exclamations were made when Ron and I started the fire. "Well, look at that! Good for you," Mom said, and while Stacy immersed herself in her drink and a book, the rest of us shared tips on how to roast our meal to perfection.

Over the next few days, mornings started with Walter's hearty pancakes topped with the wild strawberries that Mom had helped us kids gather, while afternoons were spent at the swimming hole or the nearby lake. Roger had tried to persuade Mom to go canoeing, but I was pleased when she chose instead to swim in the cool water with me and bask in the sunshine. In the evening we had more marshmallow-roasting fun. As ever, my heart was heavy when it came time to say goodbye.

Misadventures

Over the next few years we spent every long weekend, the odd weekend in between—except in the harsh winter months—and the whole
month of August at the cabin on the property, leaving the animals back
home in a neighbour's charge. At the cabin our days were more relaxing
than at home. We kids would help with the odd jobs here and there, like
sweeping the floors and banging out mats, but usually while Walter and
Stacy puttered, we were free to explore the alpine forest.

Walter would say, "Who needs Disneyland? Who needs Hawaii?
We've got all we need right here. We live in one of the most beautiful
places in the world." With rolling hills and pastures all around us, his
point was easy to see. We admired the paintbrush flowers along the trail
that led to the large Douglas fir we liked to perch in to admire the view
or nibbled on wild chives as we walked the beaten path to the summer
cabins on the other side of the river, wading in water up to our knees
as we crossed. Sometimes we'd stand stock still until trout schooled
around us and attempt to catch one bare-handed before it darted way.
All the while, we'd make plenty of noise, either talking loudly or clapping as Walter had instructed us, so we wouldn't surprise any bears. His
advice must have worked because I remember seeing only the odd bear
through the windows of the truck.

It didn't occur to us kids that anything terrible could happen in
these surroundings, but now that I think of it, it's not surprising that we
experienced a few misadventures, the Cariboo being such a vast, wild
place. One sunny afternoon while we were heading back from a family
hike, Walter agreed to let Ron take a shortcut home. We were near the
big swamp where we liked to paddle in an old rowboat we'd found, and
off my brother went through the thicket of evergreens surrounding it.
Walter had told us that if we ever lost our way we should just follow the
rushing river home, but Ron couldn't use the river to navigate because
it was on the far side of the meadow. About thirty minutes later we

arrived back at the cabin, and Ron was nowhere to be seen.

"Walter, Ron's not here," Stacy said, worried.

"Yeah, if it's a shortcut, he should have beaten us home," I said, worried as well.

"I'm sure he'll show up soon," Walter said optimistically.

"I hear something," said Pat. "Do you hear it?"

"I don't hear anything," I said.

"I hear something too," said Walter.

"You sure it's not just the wind?" Stacy asked.

"No, it's not," replied Walter.

We all heard it then. It sounded like the peacocks I'd heard in Stanley Park, but it wasn't. It was Ron yelling in the distance, "Help, help! Somebody help me!"

We glanced worriedly at one another.

"I'm coming, Ron! I'm coming!" Walter called.

Stacy, Pat and I watched helplessly as Walter went back to look for Ron. Fortunately it wasn't long before he walked into our sight down an old logging road at the edge of the meadow. He was crying quietly.

"It's okay, Ron. I'm here. You're okay," Walter assured him.

—⋘—

That fast-flowing river caused another scare. One blistering hot day, Ron and I were eager to jump into the refreshing water of the swimming hole to escape the heat. Ron swam easily across to the sandy beach on the other side, but when I ran in, the current sucked my light frame down and pinned me against a partly submerged bush. With the bush behind me and the current against me, I dog-paddled madly in an effort to get out, but my body wouldn't move.

To this day, I don't think I've ever held my breath as long as I did that afternoon. Seconds later I heard Walter arrive on the grass by the water's edge. Seeing his silhouette blurred through the window of the rapids, I shouted silently for him to rescue me, but it was a few moments before he realized what was happening and fished me out. I immediately burst into tears, and from that day forth, I had a whole new respect for the river. I would enter ever so slowly, testing the waters, and when Walter and the boys went inner tubing, I stayed with Stacy on shore, both of us immersed in books.

We kids also enjoyed taunting the bulls that roamed among the free-range cattle, and whenever one of them turned on us, we'd run like hell for safety in the snake-fenced yard that surrounded the cabin. "That was close!" we'd shout. By the time the poplar leaves had turned orange and gold our first year there, Stacy had got into her head that we needed to replace some of the rotting fence railings, and Walter and Ron set to work. They sized all the logs before going back home to tend to the animals, planning to return the following weekend to do the fence repairs. Stacy, however, was anxious to get on with the job, but the thing was, there was now only Stacy, Pat and me to do it. I was a scrawny twelve-year-old and Pat was eight.

"Come on, you guys, let's move this log," Stacy said, while she stood at one end of a twenty-foot pole about four inches thick, while Pat and I stood at the other. "Okay, on three: one, two, three, lift!" We did our best to raise the log and hold it for a few seconds while Stacy hollered at us to carry it into place, but it was heavy and I lost my grip. We dropped it, creating a nasty vibration on her end.

"What the heck did you drop it for?" she yelled.

"It's too heavy, Stacy," I said, my breathing laboured, rubbing my aching arms while Pat quietly looked on.

"Let's give it another go. It's not that heavy."

"I'm sorry, Stacy, but I just can't do it!"

"You will do as I tell you. Lift this log *now*!"

Even though I was angry and my arms were sore, I did as I was told. She counted to three, and we held that log up a few seconds before it bounced to the ground again.

"I can't lift it, Stacy. It's too heavy!" I cried.

Pat watched us holler and curse at each other for a while, before I stormed off, done with her silly idea.

One cool fall day about a month later I was visiting my friend Vicki, who lived on the neighbouring property and rode the school bus with me. We were in the bathroom together when she noticed a lump in my groin.

"What's that?" she asked, pointing.

"I don't know," I answered, embarrassed. "It's been there for a while." I'd noticed the lump days earlier and seen that, whenever I pushed on it, it would pop back out.

"Maybe my mom should take a look."

"Okay, I guess," I agreed hesitantly.

"I think it's a hernia," her mother said after gently touching the lump. Later she told Aunt Stacy, who took me to the doctor.

Vicki's mom was right. I had to have surgery months later at BC Children's Hospital. I remember Stacy and I took the train and stayed at an Easter Seals House. The next morning she complained that she had "barely slept a wink" because I had moved around so much in the bed we shared and even kicked her in the night. I didn't know what to say. Mom had never complained all the times I'd slept with her. Besides, it's not as if I knew what I was doing. I was sleeping!

Mom told me later that she'd dropped by the hospital, but her timing hadn't been good as I had just got out of surgery and was still drowsy from the anaesthetic. My poor mother. I hadn't recognized her, and I'd called her Stacy.

—✸—

The following spring when the weather was right for construction, the logs for the house, already cut to size, were hauled to the new property on a semi, followed by a truck and trailer with a large crane on board to connect them together like a puzzle. Unfortunately, although they all made it across the bridge over the river, the weight of the logs and heavy machinery caused the bridge to crack. With the bridge out, we had to take the long way back to town, turning right at the end of the driveway instead of left, the big trucks following us. The gravel road was narrow and dicey in places, but, stopping on occasion, the men scratching their heads to figure out the best way to approach the tricky sections, all the vehicles made it through. Later Walter had to place numerous phone calls to get somebody to fix the bridge. Looking back, I realize the whole ordeal must have cost him and Stacy a pretty penny.

We had misadventures back home as well around this time. I don't know who would want to break into such a dump of a house, but one Sunday night when we returned from the cabin, we found the door had been jimmied open. Our stereo had been stolen, and the freezer full of Angus beef, from one of the cows that Walter had arranged to have butchered, had been emptied.

"Who would want to steal meat?" I asked Walter.

"Well, the person must have been pretty desperate," he replied.

"Yeah, I guess."

⎯⎯⎯

It was around this time that Walter brought home a sturdy Appaloosa mare, light grey dappled with black patches, and corralled her with the cattle. She must have stood at least sixteen hands high. I was really excited because for some time I'd dreamed of having a horse, but all I could do was admire the animals from afar, either trotting in neighbouring fields or in the picture books I'd received on my birthday a couple of years back.

"She'll be a great workhorse," Walter said. "And what's a farm without a horse?" He had his dreams too and talked about using her to haul equipment on the field of hay he was going to grow at the new property to feed all the cattle he was going to own.

One cool morning beside the barn, Walter saddled and bridled the mare and then gave me a quick lesson on how to use the reins, just as his grandfather had shown him when he was a boy. But that first day I rode a horse would be the same day my childish fancy for horses died.

"Let her know you're the boss," he said. "Make sure you pull the reins with confidence."

I didn't feel confident at all. As I sat in the saddle, she pranced around, all nervous and jumpy, which was how I felt too.

"You're doing fine," Walter said. "Why don't you just walk her around a bit? Give her a gentle nudge with your knees to get her going."

Squeezing her torso lightly while Walter made clicking sounds encouraged her, all right, but she didn't walk and she didn't canter. She galloped. She took off like a bolt of lightning, and it was all I could do to stay in the saddle. I don't think she liked being ridden at all and, trying to get me off, she ran straight into the forest, weaving around trees and jumping over rotting logs.

It was a good thing I had worn my jacket because it provided a bit of protection from the branches that whipped my body and arms. The only thing I could do to protect my face and head was to duck under tree limbs and hope for the best. As I gripped the reins and squeezed my legs against her in an effort to stay on, I could hear her heavy panting and the sound of her hooves slapping the ground, and I could feel her body sweating. After a whirlwind ride of a few minutes, I was lucky she decided to return to the barn, tired and worn out.

"Are you okay?" Walter asked as he grabbed the reins.

"Yeah, I think so," I answered in shock.

"What a stupid horse! No wonder she was so cheap!"

It wasn't long before he sold her, which was fine with me. My horse phase was over. Weeks later I realized the incident could have been much worse when a spunky little girl who travelled on the school bus with us was killed after her horse was spooked and ran into traffic. She would have been only about seven years old. It was hard to believe someone could die so young. I didn't know her well, but she and her older brothers were famous for their swearing and carrying on, and when her brothers returned to the bus without her, there was a sympathetic hush for days.

—∞—

A few months before my thirteenth birthday, I made another trip to the hospital. It all started one afternoon at Vicki's place. With Stacy working as an insurance agent again, she and Walter were both in town all day. After Vicki showed off her parents' new truck, she came up with the idea of us pulling each other around the property using her dad's garden tractor with a small trailer attached.

"You know how to drive it?" I asked.

"Sure, my dad lets me drive the tractor all the time."

"Okay, I guess."

While she sat in the driver's seat, I climbed into the small, wooden trailer, stood at the front and grasped the top of the waist-high plywood walls.

"You ready?" she asked.

"Yep."

The ride was a bit bumpy but kind of cool. She drove about as fast as a car driving in a parking lot, pulling me around the dusty property for a few minutes and then stopping the tractor about twenty feet from her parents' new truck.

"You wanna try?"

I figured if she could do it, so could I. It seemed simple enough.

She showed me how to start the engine, then we switched places. The thing was, she hadn't shown me how to stop or change the gears, and I hadn't thought to ask. Next thing I knew, I was heading straight for her parents' new vehicle. I thought about cranking the steering wheel hard, but by this time I was only a few feet away.

"Stop the tractor!" yelled Vicki.

I stared helplessly at the controls, but I didn't know what button to press or what lever to pull. Seeing an impending collision, I panicked and jumped off while the tractor was in motion. When I hit the dusty ground, I felt an electric shock sensation in my foot.

"You idiot!" Vicki yelled. "You hit my parents' new truck!" I tried to walk but couldn't. My foot hung like a rubber chicken. Every time I put my weight on it, pain would shoot up my leg. Leaving Vicki to her freak-out, I hopped on one foot to the house, then slowly up a long flight of stairs to the main floor.

"Phyllis, you okay?" Vicki's mother asked. She'd been gabbing with a friend and hadn't been paying attention to what we were doing. Her friend settled me onto a chair with my limp foot resting on another chair and gingerly took off my shoe and sock.

"I think it's broken," I told her.

"I don't know. It's probably just a bad sprain," she said, gently prodding my ankle before applying ice.

"I'm pretty sure it's broken," I repeated.

Both adults disagreed with me. I think they didn't want to admit that my foot was indeed broken. An hour or so later Vicki's mother finally called Walter, but by then my foot was purple and swollen to twice its normal size. I thought that if they had listened to me in the first place, my foot would have been better off. Walter took me for X-rays, and I had to spend a couple of days in the hospital waiting for the swelling to subside enough so that my foot could be cast. I thought for sure I'd be in for it, but instead my aunt and uncle blamed Vicki's mother. "How come she didn't know what you two were up to? That's the last time you'll be going there!" Walter said.

I missed sports day, I missed my class canoe trip and I missed ever going to Vicki's house again.

Sunshine and Clouds

I had never dreamed of playing the flute. The thought had never crossed my mind. I was vaguely aware that grade seven band classes had started, but I hadn't really paid much attention. All I knew was that twice a week the students who had chosen band as their elective subject left the classroom while the rest of us did art. All that changed for me one day when a smartly dressed, grey-haired substitute teacher named Mr. White taught our class.

It was the same day our puppy, Sammy, had been hit by a car, so I was pretty upset. We'd got her only about a week earlier from the couple who rented the weathered cottage beside us. I had let her out for a tinkle, then called and called for her to come back, but finally I had to give up or risk missing the school bus. Then, as I walked to the highway's shoulder, I saw her lifeless body in the middle of the road. I called to Ron, who was just steps behind me, to wake up Uncle Walter, who came out and lifted her into the back of his truck. "That's too bad," he said, shaking his head. That day I vowed to myself I would never own a pet again as long as we lived near a busy road. (We didn't have a good track record with pets. A couple of years later we'd get two more dogs, but they disappeared too. We came home one day after a weekend at the cabin, having left them in a neighbour's charge, and they were gone.)

Word about Sammy spread throughout the class, and when Mr. White heard the sad news, he told me I could stay inside at recess if I liked. For moral support my best friend, Ursula, stayed with me. I'd noticed her weeks before, how she seemed comfortable in her own skin, always on the sidelines of the school crowds and not all drama and giggles like most of the other girls our age. Like me, she was a middle child between two boys. When our teacher had read aloud the short story she had written about butterflies fluttering in the breeze, I knew I had to get to know her. "You're a great writer," I told her at break. We'd been friends since. Practically every lunch hour we'd wander to the back field away from the crowds and sing the hymns she'd learned in church, where she went with her mother every Sunday. She had the voice of an angel, and her singing warmed my heart.

Mr. White had just finished directing our weekly recorder class before recess that day. "You're pretty good on that recorder," he told me, "and I notice that you can read the notation. You don't have the names of the notes written down like most of the other kids."

His words cheered me up a bit. I told him I had learned to read music because I didn't like the note names cluttering the page. He mentioned that his wife taught flute, and then, since he was taking such a kind interest in me, I told him I was a foster child and my uncle was the new manager at the local bank. I figured I'd never see him again, but that evening at dinner Walter told me that a fellow named White had stopped by his office and wanted to know if I'd like to take music lessons from his wife. I thought, *Why not?* "You can start on Wednesday," Walter said. "I have their address. You can walk to their place after school and I'll pick you up on my way home from work."

The following week I knocked on the door of their little white rental. I would have given it an eight even though there wasn't much colour, with the yard and what I could make out as a garden covered with a light dusting of snow, but I imagined it would look different in the spring when the grass was green and the plants were in bloom. Besides, it was quaint and tidy. I could hear dogs barking on the other side of the door.

"Oh, hello," said a trim lady in her forties with honey-coloured hair pinned up in a bun. She was wearing a brown tweed skirt and a copper-coloured blouse. "Calm down, Winston and Midget," she said gently with a British accent to the two cocker spaniels squirming and jumping beside her. "Do come in! You must be Phyllis. Don't mind the dogs. They always bark when people come over. Go lie down," she directed them gently, waving her hand. "I'm Helen. My husband, Edward, has told me all about you. You must be hungry after a long day at school. Would you like some cookies and a hot drink? Let me take your coat."

Later she would explain that she had emigrated from England, where she had trained as a nurse, and now worked shifts at the local hospital. Years earlier she had been given the opportunity to come to

Canada with her aging grandmother, who wanted to visit her sister on Vancouver Island. To the disappointment of her family, Grandma returned to England alone because Helen fell in love with the Island's quaintness and had decided to stay. She had rented a cottage in Victoria and was happy to be a vast ocean away from her "overbearing parents." She and Edward had met in Victoria and had spent many summers camping in the Cariboo countryside, finally deciding to settle there. They had recently purchased a house on acreage on the outskirts of town, which they would eventually turn into a private school, and they planned to have a log home built there before the following winter.

She hung my coat on a hook by the door and led me to the dining room, where a saucer of cookies was set on a beautiful wooden dining table. By now the dogs had settled cozily by the fireplace. When she went into the kitchen, I sat down and shyly scanned the place, which was prettily decorated with paintings, plants and warm-coloured furniture. I decided the house was definitely an eight, maybe even a nine. Everything fit together nicely like a piece of art, so different from our home, where functionality was the focus and possessions didn't seem to matter.

When she placed before me the most beautiful glass I'd ever seen, thick crystal filled with a steaming lemon drink, I was overwhelmed by all the doting and attention, and it was all I could do to thank her as she sat at the table with me, smiling warmly. "Edward tells me you're quite good on the recorder and that you can already read music, which should be very helpful for learning the flute," she said. Meanwhile, I was enjoying the cookies. She'd put out about half a dozen, but I didn't want to look greedy and ate only three of the most delicious cookies I'd ever tasted. I didn't know what they were called, but later I saw the package on the counter: French buttercreams.

After I finished the refreshments, we went into her music studio, where she showed me how to put the flute together, then demonstrated how to blow gently across the hole. I made a sound instantly, as Walter had shown me how to make a sound by blowing across beer bottles. It was the same concept. "You're a natural," she said encouragingly.

After the lesson she sent me home with a shiny flute—"because I have two," she said—and a crisp new music book filled with tunes like "Oats and Barley" and "Mary Had a Little Lamb," which I would practise and proudly play for her the following week while she filled me with positive words of encouragement.

As the months passed, my flute skills steadily improved, and it became clear that my calling had found me. I was so happy that I could create beautiful sounds, and I spent as much time practising as I could. I even took the flute to the cabin and played while on the tractor in the meadow, propping my music on the steering wheel. Walter picked up on the musical mood too: sometimes he'd whistle along while I played, and one day I heard him play a couple of his favourite folk songs on the recorder. He'd figured out the melodies by ear, then written down the names of the notes in an exercise book. It turned out that he knew the basics of music from playing the trumpet in his younger years.

—∞—

In junior high I joined the band, and it proved to be the only subject I excelled in. I wasn't great at academics. I wasn't great at sports. I wasn't great at carrying a conversation with peers, worried that I'd say too much and my foster-child identity would be revealed. But I was great at carrying a tune, and the flute became my voice. I became so confident of my skills that I played classical solos by Bach and riffs from band pieces in the hallways during lunch hour. Students and teachers would comment, "Hey, you're pretty good!"

When the band director noticed my talent, he encouraged me to join the senior band, although I was still a junior. The principal took notice too, calling me into his office one morning to tell me how well I was doing. "Keep it up!" he said.

Not used to compliments, I muttered "Thank you" awkwardly, then fled back to class.

A few weeks later Helen announced that I had passed my grade two Royal Conservatory of Music exam. I was thrilled when she handed me the envelope that had arrived in the mail, announcing, "First-class honours!" She was so proud that she arranged a write-up in the local paper.

"Tell me about your family," the lady reporter said, pen and paper in hand.

I'd told only Ursula about my foster-child identity, but now, away from my peers at school, my guard was down and I answered honestly. "Well, I don't know my father, and my mom lives in the city." I was just starting to tell her about Ron when I noticed the woman had become flustered and didn't know what to do with her pen. Helen, who was standing by, quickly intervened while I busied myself reading a poster on the town's history. Later, when I saw the article, though I was thrilled to have my picture in the paper, I was upset because the woman had written that Walter was my father and had given him my last name. She went on to write that he had "played trumpet in his high school band and his musical genes must have been passed on."

While I understood that Helen had given the reporter a simplified account of my family situation—perhaps to save me embarrassment—the message I received at the time was that the family roots that gave me my identity didn't matter. As my identity did matter very much to me, I just tucked the article that held the history of my accomplishment into my *Watch Me Grow* book.

———

After Helen and Edward had settled into their beautiful new log home—a ten—set among towering evergreens by the lake north of town, to save on travel time on my flute lesson days, I began staying overnight with them.

By this time they had become quite close friends with Walter and Stacy, inviting them to dinner and on one occasion caring for us kids while Walter and Stacy went on a week-long ski trip. Edward and Helen were happy to have us as they had married late in life and had no children together. "It was just too late to have kids," Helen had said. While Walter and Stacy were away skiing, we kids spent the days sledding on the nearby slopes and skating on the frozen lake. All three of us were comfortable on the ice, having spent hours skating on the pond by our house, but Pat and I had also taken weekly lessons when he was considering joining a hockey league. We'd walk to the arena together after school, and I'd help him tie his skates. Although I would have loved more lessons, when he decided he didn't want to play hockey anymore, they were discontinued. At Helen and Edward's home, after hours of icy entertainment, we'd warm ourselves by a campfire, roasting hot dogs and drinking hot chocolate. We also took Winston and Midget for walks along the snowy road and threw sticks for them, too, which they had fun searching for in the snow, emerging with frosty beards.

After school every Wednesday, Edward, now principal of his own private school, would pick me up in his yellow bus at the high school, where it was convenient for him to meet his private students. It wasn't long before Wednesdays became my favourite day of the week. After my flute lesson, I'd help Helen in the kitchen. I could tell she was tired at times after her long shifts at the hospital and teaching music, cooking and sewing at their school. As well as being a nurse and musician, she was a talented seamstress and used her Singer to make many of her own clothes. She performed the custodial duties for the school as well, though she never complained and always had time for a smile.

While she cooked dinner, I'd set the placemats of English ships on the dining table, then set out the silver that was kept in a fancy wooden case on the antique buffet. When dinner was ready, she'd carry out steaming meals like lamb chops, roast beef or, my favourite, toad-in-the-hole, on plates she'd warmed in the oven. Then we'd chat comfortably about the day's events.

One evening Edward told me I was "an intelligent girl." He added, "Look how easily you've taken to music. Your IQ is definitely higher than average." I couldn't remember the last time someone had told me I was smart, and I started to care more about school. Soon I was able to bring up my mediocre grades, even making the honour roll a few times, which I was proud of even if I earned mostly Bs and wasn't an A student like my friend Michelle. Even so, Walter said my report cards were "pretty good."

After our Wednesday dinners, if we weren't going for walks with the dogs or for a row on the lake, we'd retire to the living room, where on cool nights Edward would light the fireplace. We'd read or listen to blues or classical music and play Scrabble; they didn't own a television as Edward said TV rotted the mind. At bedtime I'd don the pink flannel nightgown they'd given me to keep under the pillow on the bed in the music studio.

Unlike Walter and Stacy, who liked to sleep in, Helen and Edward were always up before I was, and I would wake to the sound of CBC Radio. After dressing for the day and making my bed using the hospital corners Helen had shown me to pull the sheets tight, I'd wander into the breakfast room, where the table would be neatly set for three. After breakfast Edward would pick up the binoculars he kept on the windowsill and identify birds at the outdoor feeder that Helen or I had filled with suet. "The sparrows are hungry today," he'd say, or "The chickadees have come back early," and we'd admire the lovely creatures as they flitted by.

Helen always sent me off to school with a bagged lunch, a nice change from packing one myself all those years, and it would include either a cheese and Branston pickle sandwich or cold toad-in-the-hole, cream-filled cookies and a juicy apple. Then Edward and I would hug her goodbye, often sharing a "butterfly kiss." I'd flutter my eyelashes on her cheek, just like the gentle wings of a butterfly, then we'd giggle. As I waved to her through the bus window, she'd cheerily wave back and we'd send each other a "bluebird kiss" off the palm of the hand.

On the way to town, as Edward drove along the gravel road that ran parallel to Reed Lake and I sat on the bench seat behind, we might see a long-legged moose standing alert in the shallows while red-winged blackbirds danced in the bulrushes along the shoreline. He might comment on the charming view of the ranch by the highway turnoff, and if the land happened to be blanketed in snow, he'd say, "Looks just like a Christmas card." Often, we'd sing the Scottish folk tune he'd taught me, "The Skye Boat Song," or another favourite, "You Are My Sunshine." I'd catch his eye in the mirror above the driver's seat, he'd smile warmly and I knew the song was for me. I knew I was his sunshine.

Unfortunately Edward would become my cloud, every one of his kind acts forever shaded. One night while Helen worked the night shift, he woke me from my slumber, cradled me in his arms and carried me to the bed he and Helen shared. I was completely confused and was even more mixed up when he touched me in places he knew he shouldn't, all the while gently assuring me that we were "special friends" who held "special secrets," and returning me to my bed in the early morning.

By the time Helen arrived home, the breakfast tea was steeped and the table laid. I remember coming into the breakfast room as Helen walked in the door. Taking her coat, he said, "Come and relax with a warm of cup of tea. You must be tired." She thanked him for his thoughtfulness as they exchanged loving looks, just as they'd always done and would continue to do for years. While Helen gave an account of the busy emergency room, the morning wasn't too far different from any other Thursday. In between chatter, we sipped our tea and ate our toast, and when we left for school, we bid Helen goodbye with a hug.

I didn't want to cause an upheaval. I didn't want my music lessons to stop. I didn't want to lose Helen, *my* sunshine, whom I adored. She was like a mother to me. And Edward must have known how I felt. He knew I wouldn't tell a soul. Instead, as the months turned into years, I'd dread the calls from the hospital for Helen that for me meant *doom*. She didn't get called often, but every time the phone rang for her, off she went. While tightly clutching the covers, silently pleading that he wouldn't come for me, I'd hear the creak of the stairs, their gentle voices bidding each other goodbye and the decrescendo of the engine as Helen drove away, leaving me alone with him.

He always came. Moments after Helen left, I'd hear the swish of the bedroom door swinging open. He'd slip into the shadowy room, his silhouette hovering over me like a looming ghost. "Come, little one," he'd say and then cradle my body and carry me into darkness.

Snow, Cinnamon and Bottles

"We have running hot water and a bathroom! What more could you ask for?" Walter exclaimed after we had settled into a rented shack across the highway from our first rented shack. "Besides, it's only $300 a month!"

We kids were not impressed. It was almost exactly like the dreary home we'd left, another three, hidden behind evergreens at the end of a dirt driveway with a bunch of shabby outbuildings behind it. While we agreed it was nice not to have to use an outdoor toilet anymore, the washroom Walter was so pleased with wasn't anything to celebrate. The free-standing sink was riddled with brown spots, the toilet bowl was rusted, and the ancient bathtub was surrounded by a stained plastic curtain that hung from a rust-spotted rack. To provide the option of showering, a vacuum hose hung from the faucet, and Walter wouldn't replace it with a shower head until the day the hose fell off, scalding Pat. The one small window, like most of the windows in the place, couldn't be opened because it was covered in thick, grey plastic to keep out the frigid winter air. As there was no ventilation, black mould peppered the walls all the way down the hall to the boys' bedroom.

The state of our home's disrepair was odd, as Walter was quite the handyman, constantly puttering with his vehicles. We liked to watch him work and even help at times. "Pass me the wrench," he'd say, pausing in the middle of the tune he was whistling, and we'd happily rummage through his tool box. Being such a practical guy, he even took us to the local dump at times to find a part he needed. "The best deals in town are found at the dump," he'd say. "Who can beat free?" We'd often see opportunistic black bears prowling around the dump too, but Walter said to ignore them, that they weren't interested in us. He was right. They never paid us any mind.

Sweeping was a constant chore in this shack, as dust worked its way through the cracks in the floorboards. For months at a time I'd have a hacking cough, a stuffed-up nose and watery, sty-infected eyes, and after Helen gave me medicated cream to rub on them, they were not only swollen and red but gooey as well. With my puffy eyelids and my explosive sneezing, my schoolmates were completely disgusted by me. "Ew, gross!"

Even my best buddy, Ursula, turned away at times. Now that we were in high school, we'd sometimes walk to her townhouse for lunch. Her mom was an amazing baker. I can still smell the fresh bread and buns spread all over the counters of their bright little kitchen. I'd break open a steaming roll while she and Ursula spoke German; I didn't mind that I couldn't understand them, immersed as I was in the luscious home-baked flavours. Her mom would speak to me the odd time, too, but would lapse into German mid-sentence.

"Mama, speak English," Ursula would say. "Phyllis can't understand you."

Her father worked shifts at the mill. My only memory of him is the time I had to use the bathroom, which meant walking across the dreary living room where he sat in a ragged lounge chair drinking a beer while he watched wrestling. He grunted at me, but I never said anything back, just kept walking. Years later Ursula would say, "That's how I remember him too!"

In our new home we didn't keep cows, as Walter was likely tired of chasing them around. Instead, we had a trio of goats, two of them nannies: Cinnamon and Beth. Goats will, of course, eat anything, even the shirt right off your back, so when it was my turn to do their daily milking, I'd be sure to lure them with a bucket of oats; otherwise they'd chew on my shirt sleeves or kick over the bucket of milk I'd worked so hard to fill. I wasn't impressed when I had to milk them on my birthday. It was a rule that we didn't have to do chores on our special day, but Walter and Ron weren't around and wouldn't make it home until hours later—just in time for the birthday cake—so the job had fallen to me. "But it's my birthday!" I yelled indignantly at Stacy.

In fact, I should have let the goats knock the bucket of milk over, as I wouldn't have had to pour it over my cereal. I found the bitter taste worse than the powdered milk Mom had served. And it didn't help that breakfast was often tasteless puffed wheat with the consistency of Styrofoam. Walter would purchase huge bags of it. "They're a great deal—only five dollars!" he'd say.

The third goat, a smelly, white billy that stank of urine, was called Snowman. To tell if the nannies were in heat, he would put his nose right into their spray, then hold his head high in the air and sniff. I found it completely disgusting. These three animals wandered freely around the property, as it was surrounded by wire fencing, and they even came into the house whenever we didn't latch the door properly. They would get into the oats and flour stored in paper bags on the kitchen's open shelves, and Stacy would yell, "Get those smelly animals outta here!" We'd grab them by the neck and use all the strength we could muster to force their noses out of the kitchen grub they were enjoying, kicking and slapping them to get them out of the house. They climbed onto our vehicles too, and many days we drove to town with muddy hoofprints on the truck's hood and roof.

Soon goat kids were running around the property too. The first was white like his father, a cute bundle of romping energy. We called him Snowball. Pat was particularly enamoured of him and was filled with laughter as they romped around the yard together, but when Snowball ended up on the table, Pat was the last to laugh. "This is Snowball we're eating, you guys. How does he taste?" Walter asked after we'd gathered round the table for dinner, and we looked at him in shock. Ron and I handled the situation okay, but Pat's eyes filled with tears and he refused to eat. Walter laughed. "He's a farm animal!" he said. "What did you think we were going to do with him?"

From then on, Walter gave the baby goats names like Sirloin and T-Bone, but it took at least a month before Pat came around to eating goat. It was either that or go without meat, because goat was now our dinner mainstay. Fortunately, as Walter was the local bank manager, clients often gave him game cuts, so we had the odd meal of bear, moose, venison and even cougar.

Sometime that year we met Marie, a tall woman with mousy brown hair, who became our social worker for the next few years. I don't remember much about her as we saw her only semi-annually, though I do remember that first meeting very clearly. Ron, Pat and I were home from school as we had contracted ringworm, an itchy fungal skin infection we'd caught from the goats. She arrived with her arms full of paperwork, and since she asked if we had any homework to do, I assumed she worked for the school district. Afterwards I realized she was only concerned that we kept busy while she had her pre-arranged meeting in the kitchen with Stacy. When the teapot was empty and their chat was over, she waved a cheery goodbye.

⸺

The best thing about the second shack we lived in was the network of cross-country ski trails out back, where we made good use of the skis we had received for Christmas that year. (Walter and Stacy received additional funds from Social Services for expenditures such as sports equipment and school photos.) Skiing kept us busy for hours and gave us something to do during the long Cariboo winter. We'd pack food, don our gear and, with Ron leading the way, glide off into that winter wonderland for hours at a time.

On Easter weekend that same year, Walter started an annual scavenger hunt tradition at the cabin, keeping us busy hiking or even skiing at times when winter still held on to its grip on the land, looking for clues he'd hidden in places such as the tractor, the shed or inside long-abandoned cabins. Even though we learned our prize—a healthy stash of granola bars, carob and naturally flavoured fruit gummis—was always in our sleeping bags, we enjoyed the adventure nonetheless.

⸺

By the late winter of 1983, Stacy's belly was taking on the shape of a basketball with a baby soon expected, and Walter and Stacy held a family meeting. "We'll be expecting you to help out more," Walter said, looking to Ron and me in particular, as we were older. (We came to dread these family meetings, as they always meant there was more work to be done.) In the meantime, with a baby on the way, Stacy had to cut down on her alcohol consumption, and one evening when Walter was going to crack open a beer, she complained, "Aren't you going to support me in this?" He had to settle for apple juice.

Tony was born when the wild lilies and lupines on the outskirts of the property began to bloom, adding splashes of colour around the gravelled, muddy yard. I don't remember the exact day he arrived, but I do remember that the neighbourhood ladies threw a baby shower days before his entry into the world. We all sat in someone's living room with the mother-to-be at front and centre, everyone chattering as she opened the gifts. I also remember that after she returned home from the hospital with her newborn, her milk didn't come in, which meant Tony needed to be bottle-fed. Walter and Stacy kept prepared bottles in the fridge and showed Ron and me how to warm them in the microwave, then shake some of the milk onto our wrists to make sure it wasn't too hot. In the coming months, whenever we weren't in school and Tony was whiny and seeking food, Stacy would summon us. "Phyllis, it's time to give Tony his bottle." I would sit on the couch and gently lay him across my lap, resting his head in the crook of my elbow, while my other hand held the bottle. As he suckled, I'd feel his warmth while I admired his creamy skin, long, dark lashes and pudgy cheeks. "Don't forget to burp him!" Stacy would order.

Stacy stayed home with the new baby on the sunny weekend that spring when Walter threw a "roofing party" for the new log home on their acreage. He was very proud of his team-based idea, providing buckets of fried chicken and coolers of beer for every able-bodied friend or neighbour willing to show up at the property with a hammer, ready to work. Of course, booze mixed with rooftops made for a risky proposition, but there weren't any calamities, only some bickering, particularly between Edward and Joshua, who, with their previous building experience, each thought they knew best.

Pat and I helped down on the ground. After the men carried the bundles of shakes up the ladders, they would sometimes discover that the fit wasn't quite right and would yell down for a couple of narrower ones. We would go eagerly through the loose shakes on the ground, then pass them up the assembly line to someone perched midway on the ladder. If those shakes didn't fit, we'd rummage again and find others that did.

On another weekend the windows were installed, so that by the fall of 1983 the house was at the lock-up stage. Eventually the wiring and interior plumbing were added, and Walter and Stacy's dream home became our vacation home, with plans for the family to settle there full-time a few years down the road. The basement was unfinished and used only for storage, the main level had a living room, master bedroom, mud room, kitchen and bathroom (with a pump toilet), and the loft area had two large bedrooms complete with balconies and picture windows to admire the views. I would have rated it as an eight. It wasn't as stunning as Helen and Edward's place as it stood on a pebbly yard with no balcony railings or colourful plants, but Walter and Stacy were pleased with it. I remember them standing with their arms around each other, admiring their grand house with pride in their accomplishment.

I turned fourteen that fall. At home one evening I glanced out the kitchen window as I was washing the dishes to see Stacy sitting in the driver's seat of the Jimmy, resting her head on the steering wheel. About thirty minutes later, after I'd settled in front of the television with Walter, she came inside, didn't say a word and went straight to her bedroom. The next evening Walter and Ron squeezed Tony's crib into my room, and as Walter turned in early, he said, "Phyllis, you know what to do if Tony wakes up. Good night!"

On many nights after that, I woke to Tony's cries and got up to warm his bottle while the rest of the house slept. "Here you go, pumpkin," I'd whisper. Sometimes, while he drank greedily, I'd give him a fresh bottom as well, if the stink was too much to ignore, then I'd drift back to sleep to the sound of his sucking on his bottle. In the morning before heading off to school, I'd give him another bottle and change his disposable Pampers to a cloth diaper, making sure to carefully close the pins. I did stab him on occasion; then he'd wail and I'd guiltily apologize as I gently rubbed his poked little hip. I didn't mind helping out in this way. I didn't know any differently. He was certainly a special little boy, a perfect bundle of sweetness, and all the changing, feeding and laundering would lead me to develop a fond sisterly love for him.

With the family growing, Walter and Stacy purchased a cheap trailer for Ron, Pat and me to sleep in, placing it strategically close to the back door so that Walter could string an extension cord that would provide us with light. While I was happy to have the sanctuary of my own room again, the trailer's echoing emptiness wasn't very inviting, and as it wasn't insulated, it was very cold. I was better off than Ron and Pat, though, as their room was at the far end of the trailer, well away from the heat of the wood stove, and they often went to bed fully dressed with long johns underneath to keep warm. Having once lost our home to fire, whenever it was my turn to stoke the old wood stove with logs, I'd make sure to close the dampers so the wood would burn slowly, its warmth lasting through the night so we wouldn't freeze. Then I'd lie awake for what seemed hours, anxiously watching the fire's reflection on the walls outside the door that I kept open in order to stay warm, worried that the old stove's burnt-brown windows would shatter and cause the trailer to catch fire, and that I would perish in my sleep.

Railway Ties

During the remainder of our childhood, Ron and I would have visits with Mom twice a year: one week in summer and one week in winter. As the time for our visit approached, Walter would call her from work to set up arrangements and then later tell me, "Your Mom's fine." I realize now that he was letting me know she was stable. On one occasion he added, "You know, after you guys moved west, I used to look after you when your mom was in hospital. Ron was easy. As long as he had a bottle, he was happy as a clam. But you, you were inconsolable! You'd cry for hours." Then he chuckled. I didn't think this was funny at all; I had been a tot missing my mother, so of course I had cried.

Over the next few years, he never visited his sister, but he and Stacy would take us to the train station so we could travel to the Coast and meet Mom at the terminus in North Vancouver. We'd keep ourselves occupied on the trip with reading, listening to our Walkmans or admiring the sights. In summer we'd witness the gathering of hundreds of eagles along the Cheakamus River for the salmon run. In winter we'd gaze out at snow-covered pastures and watch dots of skiers descending from the frosty peaks of Blackcomb and Whistler.

Although our visits with Mom weren't long, we always made the most of our time together. While Walter and Stacy now dealt with the day-to-day routines in our lives, Mom became our fun parent. We had our first summer visit in the year I was twelve, and I remember Roger and Ron heading out to visit the pawnshops in Vancouver. Before leaving, Roger went through a box of Mom's records looking for something to pawn while she stood by, making sure he didn't take her favourites. She had classic Beatles singles like "Twist and Shout," "Help" and "Hey Jude," LP albums by the Monkees and Jim Croce and other, lesser-known artists like Nana Mouskouri. On later visits, sometimes she'd put on a record and, depending on the artist, Ron and I would find a way to groove and lip-synch in her tiny apartment while she looked on, smoking and laughing. Her favourite was the Canadian legend Anne Murray. "Just don't take any of my Anne Murray records," she told Roger that day. "Don't you dare touch those!"

Roger had then gone on about his own favourite artist, Elvis, the best rocker of all, "the true king of rock 'n' roll," gyrating his hips as he sang, "You ain't nothin' but a hound dog, cryin' all the time ..."

After they departed for the pawnshops, I discovered some Crimplene dresses and floppy hats from the sixties and seventies in Mom's hall closet. "Hey, Mom? Why don't you ever wear any of these dresses anymore?" I asked.

"Those old things? I don't really have anywhere to wear them," she said.

"Can I try them on?" I'd asked, thrilled with my discovery.

"Suit yourself."

While listening to Anne Murray sing hits like "Daydream Believer" and "You Needed Me," I tried on a scratchy yellow dress with a sparkling, swirling design, applied makeup and costume jewellery, added a floppy hat and chunky heels, then swaggered around, admiring myself in the mirror, trying to stay upright. "How do I look, Mom?" I asked, and she smiled and told me the outfit looked better on me than on her.

Our Deer Lake tradition continued. I remember, on that visit, lying on a blanket after a dip in the lake, doing a crossword beside Mom, who was smoking her usual handmade cigarettes. Every time I was stuck for a word, I'd read out clues, and she, Roger and Ron would either pitch in with the word or decline, not knowing the answer either. At one point I glanced at Oakalla Prison across the lake and wondered fleetingly if Uncle Jack was out of prison yet.

The biggest challenge on our visits to her tiny apartment was finding room for all of us to sleep, not to mention finding privacy. We'd take turns changing in the bathroom after first asking, "Does anyone need the washroom?" But Mom had our sleeping quarters figured out. Ron slept on a makeshift bed in the entry hallway, using the cushions off the couch held together by a twin sheet. Roger slept on the cushion-less couch, while Mom and I slept in the double bed, spooning together like old times. Sometimes she'd scratch my back with her sturdy, long nails, unlike mine, which were bitten short.

"Just a little lower, Mom," I'd say.

"There, is that better?" she'd ask.

"Oh, yeah, now a bit to the left." Who doesn't like a good back scratch? She scratched all of our backs.

With our circumstances changed, Mom started new traditions. One of them was giving Ron and me spending money, forty dollars each, to make up for the birthdays and other special occasions we'd missed spending together. Years later I learned that our impoverished mother skipped meals for months in order to put on a good showing when we visited.

We always went clothes shopping, taking the bus to the nearest mall or walking to the Salvation Army on Columbia Street. Mom never bought anything, but I remember her face lighting up when we found something we fancied among the racks of clothes. We'd help Roger search for his purchases, too, usually for his signature wardrobe—denim shirts, blue jeans and black leather platform boots, even in the summer heat.

Mom and Roger used their discount bus passes, but Ron and I had to pay. It must have been the year I turned thirteen that a bus driver told us we hadn't paid enough.

"What do you mean?" Mom demanded. "It's seventy-five cents for students and that's what they paid."

"Well, they need to show their Go cards then," the driver said.

"Go cards? What's a Go card?" Mom asked, her voice getting louder.

"A student card. They should have them."

Ron and I looked at each other.

"Well, they don't live here, so they don't have them, but they're students," Mom said.

"I'm sorry, ma'am, but if they don't have Go cards, they're going to have to pay the full rate."

Now Mom was angry. "What do you mean they have to pay the full rate? It's obvious they're student age. That's ridiculous!"

While it didn't make sense that Ron and I had to pay more, Mom making a scene embarrassed us. "It's okay, Mom. Granny sent some money," Ron said, fumbling for the change. "We'll pay the extra. It's not that much more."

"Yeah, Mom, it's no big deal," I agreed. "We have some money."

While I could tell she wasn't too happy with us paying more than what she figured was fair, she calmed down. Even though her money situation seemed better these days, I knew things weren't easy for her. As part of a school assignment earlier that spring, I'd written, "When I grow up, I am planning to live with my mother. I want to be a teacher." While I hadn't given too much thought to a career choice until then, I appreciated the encouraging ways of teachers like Miss Brown and Miss McMynn. Later, back at the apartment, when I told my mother my intention to help her, I could tell she didn't believe me.

"That right?"

"It's true, Mom. I'm going to take care of you," I repeated.

"Well, we'll see," she said.

It was as if she knew something I didn't. Now I understand her wariness. She knew I carried the idealism of a child unable to grasp the size of my commitment. And I think she had received so little support for so many years that she had learned to expect very little even from me, her own daughter.

Another tradition Mom started that summer was taking us out for a meal, which was a real treat. Not even Walter and Stacy took us to restaurants, other than the odd fast-food place. I remember them taking us through the White Spot drive-through when we still lived in the city. Ron was allowed to order a burger off the regular menu, while Pat and I had to settle for Pirate Pak kids' meals, which was fine for Pat because he was seven, but I was eleven!

With Mom we always went to the Old Spaghetti Factory, which was good value because meals came with a drink, salad and spumoni ice cream. One evening, after our food had arrived and the rest of us were tucking in, she reluctantly looked at her plate of lasagna.

"What's wrong, Mom?" I asked. "Aren't you hungry?"

"How do I know it's safe to eat?" she asked.

"It's a restaurant, Mom. Of course it's safe to eat," I replied, thinking it was an odd thing to say. Roger and Ron were already going on about how good their meals were.

"How do I know they didn't put any poison in it?"

"Look up there, Mom, out the window," Ron said, distracting her.

As she turned away, he pulled her plate to his side of the table.

"There's nothing—hey, where did my dinner go?"

"I thought you didn't want it, so I took it. I'll eat it if you don't want to," he said in fun.

"All right, all right, give me my dinner back!" After that, she tucked in and ate her dinner.

For years Mom took us to the Playland amusement park too. She couldn't afford day passes, but she bought enough tickets for us to go on a few rides each, and our entry fees were covered by the coupons we received with our report cards in June. Ron and I always went on the Tilt-A-Whirl and the Music Express, both spinning rides that made me feel as if my body would be sucked right out of the seat, but we screamed with glee at the top of our lungs while Roger and Mom grinned from the sidelines. My favourite rides, however, were the ones Mom and I did together. We always went on the Ferris wheel, admiring the view from the top and waving to Roger and Ron below as our chairs swung back and forth. And we all enjoyed the bumper cars. "I'm coming to get you!" we'd yell, giggling as we bumped and crashed. Usually when we returned to Mom's apartment after our excursion, she would declare she needed a nap, which I see now was her way of coping. She and Roger would spoon on the bed, I'd lose myself in a book, and Ron would listen to his Walkman.

Mom did her best to make our Christmas visits special. We didn't celebrate with her on the actual day anymore, and there were no more gatherings at Granddad's place, even though he lived only thirty minutes away, but she and Roger always waited until after we arrived to recognize the holiday. She would set up a miniature tree decorated with silver garlands and colourful baubles. To add seasonal spirit, I'd play carols on my borrowed flute; she would comment that I was "pretty good," and I'd tell her how great a music teacher Helen was.

On New Year's Eve she'd prepare a large chicken complete with all the fixings. Ron would hang around the kitchen as he always did when she cooked, a starving teen looking for a morsel, and she'd playfully slap at his quick hands, exclaiming, "Go on! Get outta there!" For dessert she always served mince pie, which Ron and I despised, but we ate it heartily anyway because she had spent so much time making it. Often Ron would even choke down seconds. But the eggnog she made was perfect, not too rich and sweet like the store-bought stuff, which didn't make much sense because she made it with tasteless powdered milk. After our feast we'd gather in front of the television to watch *Dick Clark's New Year's Rockin' Eve* while enjoying a glass of the best eggnog ever.

—∞—

One afternoon during our summer visit with Mom when I was fourteen, she suddenly said, "God speaks to me, you know." I had just finished practising my latest piece, "Sicilienne" by Gabriel Fauré, and was carefully placing the cleaned-out flute in its case. She was doing a last bit of tidying up from the previous day's family movie night. I remember that after the movie we had watched the eleven o'clock news, and Ron and I had been surprised by a rare outburst of emotion from Mom. The announcer was interviewing an older lady, a politician, who was saying something about how she cared for children and families across the province. "Yeah, right, she cares!" Mom had said. "I'd like to give her a piece of my mind." Minutes later there was a clip about Princess Diana and her latest charity work. "Now that's someone who cares," Mom said. "She doesn't put on any airs. She knows she's just a person like the rest of us." Mom loved Princess Diana, as I did. Years earlier I had snuck out of my room in the middle of the night to watch Charles and Diana's wedding on television.

Now we were preparing to head to Roger's place in downtown Vancouver. He and Ron had spent the day at the pawnshops, and he'd called earlier to suggest we go to the Old Spaghetti Factory in Gastown for dinner rather than the one in New Westminster. He didn't have a phone so he must have used a pay phone.

"What do you mean, God speaks to you?" I asked.

"Over the radio, he talks to me."

"That doesn't make any sense, Mom."

"Well, he does, you know. He tells me things."

"What do you mean? That's crazy!"

"Maybe it's because I have schizophrenia."

This was too much for my mind to fathom. I had to escape the conversation, so I went into the bathroom to get away. Fussing with my hair, I attempted to process my mother's words, asking myself in the mirror, "What is schizophrenia?" I knew my mother took medication. I saw the pills she swallowed with coffee and then chased with a cigarette. I was old enough to understand that something about her behaviour was the reason we couldn't live with her as well as the reason she couldn't earn even a modest living. Realizing that Mom was waiting for me so we could catch the bus, I walked into the kitchen. She wasn't talking about God anymore. She was placing a large carving knife in her purse.

"What are you doing, Mom? You can't put a knife in your purse!"

"Well, it's just in case. You never know."

"Seriously, Mom, you shouldn't do that."

"It'll be all right."

I was at a loss as to what more I could say to dissuade her, and we left her apartment.

I remember feeling out of place as we walked along Granville Street with its tattoo parlours, skate stores and pawnshops. There were people from all walks of life here, the kind of folk I never saw in the Cariboo: purple-haired people dressed in black leather and bedraggled beggars carrying paper cups. While Mom looked straight ahead, just like the other pedestrians who didn't pay any attention to the people around them, I could hardly tear my eyes away from a particularly unkempt lady with intense eyes, who was muttering gibberish as she sat on the sidewalk, leaning against a building on the corner. She seemed completely unaware of her surroundings, talking with her hands, trying to get her point across to some invisible person. At one point she called out as she slammed her fist on the pavement. It was very disturbing. I didn't make the connection then that my mother could become as unsettled as this deeply troubled woman, who likely needed to be in a place of care rather than on the streets.

I was relieved to arrive at Roger's place, but there it dawned on me why he spent so much time at Mom's and why he wanted to move in with her, though she turned him down every time. It wasn't just for her company, her home-cooked meals and the fact that she shaved him and clipped his nails. It was to escape the dump that he called home, which was a tiny room in a dingy downtown hotel. Mom's bachelor pad was a palace compared to this, even with its tar-yellow walls from all the smoking she did. At least she cleaned them from time to time, turning them back to creamy white. I remember her asking one day, "How do the walls look? I just cleaned them up."

While her place was peaceful with its well-insulated walls and large windows, plus a beautiful park out the back, his room was dark and dirty with one tiny window near the ceiling. There was barely room for a dresser and a single bed. A miniature television was perched on top of the dresser, clothes were scattered over the floor, and the bed was unmade. When Mom asked if anyone needed to use the washroom because we still had a few blocks to walk to the restaurant, Ron said he was fine. I thought it was a good idea, and I walked down the gloomy, creaky hallway to the shared bathroom, but after taking in the stained brown toilet, rusty sink and dirty floor, not to mention the stench, I changed my mind.

After that, the four of us headed to the restaurant, talking about the pawn deals Roger and Ron had made. Then we enjoyed our dinner seated in a refurbished train car, appreciating its novelty. As I lay in bed that night, I thought it was no wonder Roger was depressed. If I had to live in a cramped, dingy place like that, I'd be depressed too.

⸺⸺

Sometime during our visits with Mom, she always asked how Walter and Stacy were treating us. We would assure her they treated us fine and talked about our friends at school or our adventures at the cabin. It was the same whenever Walter and Stacy asked about our city visits. We'd give a short summary, with Walter usually commenting that he was glad his sister was well and that we had enjoyed our visit, while Stacy just smiled and nodded. As time passed, I understood that, as Stacy never asked after my mother directly, she had never liked her, though I think it's safe to say that Mom didn't think very highly of her either.

On the day each visit came to an end, we'd wake early to catch the train. Mom made sure to wake us on time, though I don't know how she did because she never used an alarm clock. "I don't need one," she'd say. "I can wake up early when I want to." And that seemed to be true because we were never late for our early morning boarding. We would arrive at the station and get our tickets and bags sorted, then exchange hugs and kisses, milking every moment, boarding the train at the last minute and frantically waving a teary goodbye to her and Roger from the window. "Over here, over here!" we'd shout as if they could hear us, willing them to look our way until their faces lit up in recognition and they'd wave back, easing our anxiety. As the train gradually gained speed, they'd shrink to the size of ants, and all the while we'd wave until they disappeared from view, not to be heard from or seen again for months.

It bothers me now that we didn't exchange phone calls or letters between visits. It seemed my life was like the train we travelled in: I stepped out of one compartment of my life into another.

FAMILY REUNIONS

The next couple of years were a blur of diapers and bottles. Another baby was born the summer of 1984. I remember holding Tony up to the nursery window at the hospital to see his red-faced sibling wrapped in blue. "There's Theo, your new brother!" Now that there were two of them, they were often lumped together and simply called "the boys." Time to dress the boys. Time to change the boys. Time to feed the boys. We'd moved into a rundown rancher in town by this time, a five, the first house in eons above a three. The best thing about it was its electric heat, so my fears of going up in smoke at last disappeared. And I appreciated that there were no animals to tend either. Instead we had a pair of infants to care for. Chubby Tony, sleeping through the night now, still shared a room with me, while whenever his wee brother woke early, Stacy would carry him, bottle in hand, to Ron's room, saying, "It's your turn now."

With the new additions, family get-togethers became paramount. When Ron and I took our semi-annual trip to the city that summer, for the first time in years we visited our grandfather. This must have pleased Walter as he had been complaining lately that we hadn't seen him in a long time. "He travels all over the province attending Masonic meetings but can't be bothered to visit his own family!" But Walter had to wait more than a year before Grandfather and his wife, Joan, made the trek north, cooing to the boys by day and staying in the fanciest hotel in town by night. Walter proudly showed off the new log house before Granddad and Joan headed home again.

On this summer visit, Granddad picked us up at Mom's. They had apparently kept in touch over the years, and she told me he took her for lunch once or twice a year. His picture was perched on her end table. "Hi, Carolyn," he said when he came in that day. "My, the kids have grown. How have you been keeping?" He made no move toward her for a hug or even a handshake.

Ron and I were thrilled when he and Joan took us to the orca show at the Vancouver Aquarium. Rather than imagining the show from the outside as we had all the times Mom had taken us, we could clap and cheer from the bleachers as the whales splashed the crowd with their amazing leaps and tricks. Granddad took us to a Vancouver Whitecaps game too, and Ron was particularly excited as he was playing league soccer by that time. "Did you see that kick? What an amazing goal!" The rest of our time was spent eating the endless meals that Joan prepared and watching the Summer Olympics on television.

One afternoon, while Ron and Joan were poolside, Granddad and I went to get some drinks, and he talked about the day he'd become smitten with my grandmother in small-town Manitoba. She was stepping off a wagon as he rode his horse nearby. "You have her small build," he said as he mixed a container of juice. "Your mother does too. Gosh, I wish I knew what happened to your mom. Your granny and I did the best we could, you know. When she was a teenager in the hospital, she had electroshock therapy. We thought it would help, but I don't think it did." I know now that he was referring to my mother's first committal to a psychiatric hospital. With a hint of remorse in his voice and his eyes to the floor, my grandfather added quietly, "People do the best they can with the skills they have at the time."

Although I'd never heard of electroshock therapy, I appreciated that he had been expressing care and concern for my mother, the daughter he felt he'd lost. After a few moments of silence, we locked eyes, and I could see his regret. I nodded to give him a sense that I understood, though I can't say I did, then we headed downstairs with the juice and cups, continuing with our summery, splashy afternoon.

While I am sure my grandparents had been trying to help my mother, a lump formed in my throat when I called Aunt Lynn years later. "They left her there, Phyllis," she told me. "They just left her in the mental hospital for months! And she was only fifteen! By the time she'd been released, she'd lost a year of school, her friends had moved on, and kids made fun of her because she was behind."

Months later, Walter and Stacy gave me my very own flute for Christmas. (They had received $170 from Social Services to cover the cost.) I remember us all sitting round the tree while Walter, wearing an elf hat, handed me the gift to open. My heart raced when I saw the size and shape of the parcel, thinking this was going to be the best gift ever. Once I'd peeled off the wrapping, there it was, a rectangular black box with two silver latches! My fingers were shaking with the excitement of it all. I could hardly wait. Click, click! I opened the case and gently swung the lid up. That's when my heart broke.

The best thing about my new instrument was the case with its red velvet lining. The flute, if you could even call it that, was dull, grey and chunky, not sleek or shiny at all. It looked as though it was made from the same metal as one of the cans of chicken soup I'd open when I made lunch for the boys. "Do you like it? We got it from Sears," Stacy said. With most of the eyes in the room upon me, I swallowed the lump in my throat. Somehow I was able to muster up the words "Yeah, it's great! Thank you!" without pouring my heart out all over the carpet.

Later I pretended to show my appreciation by playing melodies in my room with the door open so all could hear. The tone was horrible—not rich and warm but hollow and tinny. They say it's a poor musician who blames her instrument, but I would argue that this was an exception.

Fortunately, when my band teacher saw my pathetic instrument, he looked into my troubled soul, walked into his office, shut the door and called Helen. Before long I had a flute just like the one I'd been borrowing from her all those years. The other instrument was sent back, and I had my "musically ever after."

—•—

A month or so later, Ron, Pat and I balked when Walter and Stacy told us they planned to move the family to their new log house. Ron and I asked how we would finish school away out there in the bush. Thankfully they agreed to postpone their plans until after we graduated, and Stacy found employment designing government make-work programs instead, hiring a nanny to watch the boys until we older kids got home from school each day. Around the same time, Walter and Stacy called another family meeting with the same message as last time: we would all have to help out more. Their eyes fell as usual on Ron and me. Before long, we moved *again*, this time into a two-storey house in a middle-class neighbourhood at the edge of town. A seven, it was the nicest place we'd lived in since leaving the Coast.

Once Stacy had her first proposal ready, a chopstick factory, Walter prepared one of his popular chili dinners, and as we ate, she and Walter excitedly asked us older kids what we thought of her plan. Stacy was back to drinking again and was nursing a mug of wine, which she seemed to prefer now over a glass. I couldn't decide whether this was because she was trying to hide her drinking, whether she was worried the boys would knock over and break the delicate glass or whether she'd switched to a mug because it held more. Not wanting to bring down the energy in the room, I agreed with what they seemed to think was a great and novel idea, even though I thought it was strange that a ranching town would be creating what I viewed as Asian cutlery.

About this time Social Services stopped paying Walter and Stacy the "special rate" for fostering us, as we were no longer considered to have special needs. Ron and I were already very frugal, as by this time we had been buying our own clothes for months. Now Stacy hired Ron at minimum wage to clean her office in town once a week, which helped him buy the latest fashions. He liked the *Miami Vice* look and dressed in cool pastel colours. Fortunately she also arranged for me to babysit a brother and sister down the street, and occasionally I spent a day and a night there and got paid fifty dollars! I had my weekly allowance, too, which would have been about five or ten dollars. I still couldn't afford the latest styles, like the tie-dyed jeans the other girls were wearing, but living in town made it easy to thrift shop. I remember being teased only once about my clothes when a girl made fun of my second-hand velour shirt while we were changing after gym class. I ignored her comments. She had looked to the other girls to join in her put-downs, but they showed no interest. She never bothered me again.

⸺

The summer before I turned sixteen, a family reunion was planned to take place at Granny's getaway cabin in Quebec. The last reunion we had attended was with Stacy's side of the family in the city a few years earlier. I remember sitting in her parents' motorhome, innocently watching a family drama unfold as words were said and backs were turned. That was the last I saw of them. I was excited about this trip, although I barely remembered Granny, and we kids had never met our cousins. We'd only seen their images in school pictures. Apparently the oldest girl, Bobby, was my age, the middle child, Donald, was the same age as Pat, and the youngest was Paul, who had just started school. We talked about the trip for weeks ahead of time, wondering what they were like and if we'd get along.

As it was such a special trip (so special that Walter and Stacy received an additional $400 to help with travel costs), I used the weekly allowance I'd saved and the babysitting money I'd earned to buy a 110 camera. It didn't take too long to save up for it once I learned to avoid Walter's fining me a dollar each time Tony cussed. The little guy was at the parroting stage, and we older kids would forget to watch our language. At times he'd run around the house yelling, "Fuck, fuck, fuck …" Walter wasn't pleased, but when he told us older kids of his plan to fine us, there was no more of that.

With Tony and Theo both toddlers now, Walter purchased a minivan for the trip, bolted their car seats to the floor and attached a trailer hitch so we could pull a tent trailer and camp along the way. The boys and their parents would use the tent trailer while Ron, Pat and I would sleep in a tent. The day we left, as we drove out of town, Walter exclaimed, "You guys are really lucky! There are not many Canadians who can say they've been across Canada. Most people don't take the time to notice our splendid country and take expensive holidays elsewhere."

Stacy agreed. "It's going to be a great adventure!"

It was hotter than usual that summer and wildfires had already started, so we all cheered once we'd snuck Ron out of town to avoid having him drafted for fire duty; he was now seventeen and had just taken a fire safety course. On the road, we travelled in the cool of the morning and set up camp by late afternoon, not only to avoid the heat of the day but also because the boys always woke early so it was easier to get going while they were at their happiest. Eventually the crying and whining would start, and then it was up to the three of us in the back to keep them content, making silly faces, singing and playing peekaboo. If that didn't work, Stacy had a stash of snacks and toys for us to divvy out.

Among my memories of the trip were the towering Rocky Mountains, the flat, windy fields of Alberta, the grasshoppers of Saskatchewan and the friendliness of the people of Manitoba, just as their licence plates promised. One night we kids didn't even bother to set up our tent, choosing to bed down in our sleeping bags on a sandy lakeshore, talking in whispers while gazing at the stars and contemplating life and all its mysteries in the galaxies beyond. But the last day of our three-day drive across Ontario was one of my most memorable of the trek east, mainly because I found peace. That afternoon we had set up camp near Wawa beside a small lake and practically had the place to ourselves. While Walter and Stacy cleaned up after dinner, we older kids entertained the little boys by burying their legs in the sand until Walter suggested we go for a dip before sundown.

Ron and Pat cooled off quickly and returned to our campsite, but I was "the fish of the family," as Walter liked to say, and I swam to the middle of the lake to get away from them all. I became my own little boat, looking skyward as I imagined drifting past white cloudy islands in the pale blue sky. I lost all track of time. I could hear the water softly lapping the shore, the gentle wind rustling the leaves, the chattering of birds and soft, distant voices as I breathed in the fresh, warm air and felt the cool pillow of water beneath me. I drifted in my dreamboat world for quite some time before I heard my name in the distance. "Phy-llis! Phy-llis!" Aunt Stacy.

I wished I could ignore her, but I knew that wouldn't be a good idea, so I reluctantly swam back to shore. I'd like to say she greeted me with a smile and asked how the water was, but I'd been gone a long time. "What have you been doing? I need you to change the boys and get them ready for bed!"

⸺

Granny's cabin turned out to be more of a house than a cabin, with several bedrooms, plumbing and electricity. It was set on a patch of lawn in the woods at the end of a gravel road, not far from the lake and a short walk to the local store. From the outside I pegged it as a seven and a half, with its colourful rose bushes and rhododendrons in bloom along each side.

I remember the thrill of seeing her standing on the porch to welcome us. "Just look at you," she said as I ran toward her. "If I saw you on the street, I wouldn't even recognize you!" I was thinking the same about her, though I knew better than to say so. She'd put on weight and didn't have much hair, but Walter had told us earlier to be prepared, that she might look different because she was going through chemotherapy.

"And look at these youngsters!" she exclaimed, Theo in Stacy's arms and Tony holding Walter's hand. "Do they play shy?"

"They'll warm up eventually," Stacy said proudly.

"Come inside and meet Dennis. He built this cabin with his own two hands, you know."

Her husband, Dennis, was sitting at the kitchen table, and I could see that he was really old, much older than Granny. I could also see as plain as day that the floor was slanted, not even at all. You could literally take a ball, place it in a corner and it would roll to the opposite corner of the kitchen. I know this because we kids tried it when the adults weren't around. The ball ended up in the same corner every time. And we would soon discover that every room was like that, not square or even at all. We didn't dare mention this crookedness to Granny, though, as she was so proud of her husband's work.

But Granny sure liked to complain about my grandfather, and I realize now that she blamed him for my mother's illness. With both of us early risers, we took the opportunity while the rest of the household slept to catch up on the years we'd lost. In between minding the boys, I'd tell her about school or visits with Mom, and every so often something I said would cause a reaction. "Your grandfather was never around, you know. He was more interested in his friends than his family. If he wasn't working, he was at the golf course or at the various clubs he belonged to. And when he was around, he would get mad at your mother for singing, just for singing, Phyllis! Can you imagine? Can't a child sing?"

It wasn't until I was writing these pages that I contacted Aunt Lynn about this, and she told me that when her dad came back from the war, he was very angry. "You know he served in the war?" No. "He didn't see any action. He was a radio operator. But a lot of his friends died. Your mother, being the oldest, took the brunt of his anger, but I think she had the cells to be sick." We went on to discuss the fact that when Mom was six, she had developed encephalitis, an inflammation of the brain, as a complication of measles. Aunt Lynn continued, "And when the family lived in Manitoba, she was raped by an older neighbourhood teen. She was about thirteen at the time. She didn't tell us until we lived in Ottawa. She heard on the news that the same guy had raped another girl, and she took a knife and cut up a bush in the garden. I think that was the trigger for schizophrenia. After she got sick, Dad was ashamed of her. But I think her anger scared him too."

When our conversation was over, I turned into a puddle. I not only had a deeper understanding of the distant relationship my mother had with her father, but also began to understand her fear of men and all the warnings she had given me about men throughout my childhood.

But it wasn't just my grandfather that Granny went on about at that family reunion. She took runs at Aunt Stacy too. "I don't know why Walter stays with that woman," she said. "She was such a selfish girl. I told him she wasn't good for him, but of course he didn't listen." Stacy must have known how Granny felt because she spent most of our visit in the camper where she bunked with Walter and the boys. Granny complained about that too. "She can't even socialize with the family. Is it too much to ask to be friendly?"

Fortunately my grandmother wasn't all complaints. One morning she said that she was proud of Ron and me, that she had worried about us when we were younger, but that we were turning out really well. "I would have taken you in, you know, but I was too old. It wasn't an easy decision. Actually, when your mother was pregnant with you, your grandfather and I tried to convince her not to have you, and we told her she should have an abortion. She was already struggling to look after Ron, and your dad wasn't much help. We were worried how she'd manage. She would have nothing of it, though. She was determined to keep you, and I'm glad she did. You've grown into a beautiful girl."

At the mention of my father, part of me wanted to ask about him. Not that I had thought about him much over the past years, but this trip had brought him to the forefront of my mind. I had let myself think that I might actually see him, as he lived only hours away, but then I'd chase such thoughts away. Too much time had passed and it was better to let him go. But after Aunt Lynn and her family arrived and we went with them to Ottawa, where we toured the Parliament Buildings, I secretly scanned every middle-aged man in the crowd in search of a redhead.

In the meantime, my stomach was filled with butterflies, a mixture of excitement and anxiety: the excitement of seeing my mother, who was due to arrive that evening, and the anxiety of seeing Uncle Jack, who was due to arrive with her in Granny's car. I hadn't even known he was out of prison, and I could hardly move when he and Mom entered the room together. Somehow I found the strength to send him a nod while my mother hugged me tightly. He looked completely different, not the stocky, boisterous man I remembered but thin, shy and nervous, and I wondered if he remembered what he'd done.

Now that the family reunion was complete, excited chatter filled Granny's kitchen.

"My goodness! It's been too long!"

"How have you been?"

"Look at the children! My, they've grown!"

"Let's take a look at you!"

"That little youngster sure looks like his grandfather!"

Even though I wanted to visit with Mom, I couldn't stay in the same room with Uncle Jack, and watching them making light conversation as if he hadn't violated me all those years ago was too much to take. Leaving Granny to her tears of joy as the adults reminisced, I removed myself to the living room, where the older cousins had gathered, and we talked about pop bands in between watching television.

As the days passed, I felt a twinge of jealousy. I wished that I could have had a piece of the comfortable family memories my cousins had. Thinking about it, it seemed odd that Granny had moved our family of three to the West Coast all those years ago and left us there when she returned east a few years later. But Aunt Lynn explained, "She couldn't have known her marriage wouldn't last. When it ended, she went back to Ottawa to work for the federal government because the pay was better than keypunching. She also missed long-time friends and likely needed their support after the marriage breakdown. I would have taken you myself when your mother got sick, but Granny wanted you stay in BC to be near your mom. That's why Uncle Walter took you." After that conversation I felt a swell of emotion, realizing that if it hadn't been for my grandmother, Ron and I may have been put up for adoption and possibly separated because, according to my mother's documents, the Ontario Children's Aid had been about to intervene. Granny had kept us in the family and made sure we kept in touch with our mother.

The family visiting really began after the Ottawa trip, but I was relieved that Uncle Jack only visited with Walter and Stacy and even more relieved when he left the next day. Meanwhile, Ron and I had fun in the canoe with Aunt Lynn's daughter, Bobby, while Bobby's younger brothers joined Pat swimming around the dock. Mom and Lynn took a dip too, and later I proudly showed off my new flute, wowing everyone with a house concert.

Then one morning at breakfast when the other adults weren't around, Lynn and Stacy exchanged heated words. We were about to go to the waterslides, and Lynn had wanted to leave early to beat the rush, but Stacy had other plans.

"Walter and I are leaving with the boys tomorrow to see my half-siblings, and I need Ron and Phyllis to clean the van," Stacy had said.

"Can't they do it when we get back? It would be good to get to the waterslides before it gets too busy."

Aunt Stacy threw Lynn a dirty look, and we children exchanged nervous glances, barely breathing. The room was dead quiet.

"Well, I guess we'll just have to wait then," said Aunt Lynn, giving in.

Fortunately the wait that day turned out to be worth it. After Ron and I had cleaned out the fast-food boxes and other soggy remains from around the boys' car seats, we set off for the slides and had a great time. It was a cloudy day, but we didn't mind. We were at the waterslides! When Aunt Lynn and family left the following afternoon, along with Walter, Stacy, Pat and the boys, leaving Ron and me to have carefully planned quality time with our mother, Lynn and I cried. We were going to miss each other. It was too bad, we agreed, that we lived so far apart.

The next day, while Granny and Dennis went to a medical appointment downtown, Mom, Ron and I were happy to spend time at the mall. She helped me choose a pair of earrings, and Ron and I bought backpacks for school. Afterwards we saw the movie *Back to the Future*, laughing heartily at the twisted plot line. I was a big fan of Michael J. Fox, who starred as Marty McFly, and had a *Teen Beat* poster of him on my bedroom wall. The fun-filled day ended with a pizza dinner at Uncle Jack's apartment, where I put on a brave face while questions swirled in my head.

On our last day together, I made a vanilla cake with chocolate fudge icing for Mom's birthday, and later, after everyone else had called it a night, she and I sat at the kitchen table and talked about girl stuff.

"You have a boyfriend yet?" Mom asked, her leg kicking back and forth while she took a drag on her cigarette.

"Nah. I liked a guy named Marc for a while."

"What about your menses? Have you started?"

"Yeah," I answered, feeling uncomfortable as trips to the drugstore to buy Kotex flashed through my mind. I always scanned the shop to make sure nobody from school was around, hurriedly walked to the cashier, then quickly hid the package in my backpack.

"You know you can have a baby now, right?"

"Yeah. We learned that stuff at school."

"You be careful with those boys. They're only after one thing, you know."

I knew more than she realized, but there was no way I could tell her about Edward.

"You're growing up to be quite the young woman."

I may have been a young woman, but the next morning when it came time to bid her and my grandmother goodbye, I cried like a baby. My tears dried up only when Walter and Stacy kicked off our ten-day journey home with a surprise trip to Canada's Wonderland in Toronto. While Walter and Stacy pushed the boys in strollers, Ron, Pat, and I spent the humid afternoon taking in the many exciting rides. From there, for a change of scenery, we headed back to BC through the northern United States, though it took hours to get to our first night's campsite as Walter took a wrong turn in an attempt to avoid passing through Detroit.

The rest of our journey included staying in a drab park in Wisconsin, a crowded campsite in Minnesota and a couple of nights in the Dakota badlands, where Walter told us cowboy movies had been filmed. In the town of Medora, Walter offered to watch the boys while Stacy and I had some girl time. I remember taking up his offer with uncertainty, but she seemed cheerful enough while we wandered around the town, though our conversation was stilted and never went beyond tables and bar stools.

From there, it was on through Montana and Idaho and the burning forests of Washington State, where we were so close to the wildfires that we could feel the heat of the flames. By then, as I hadn't had a shower in days, I had a sty outbreak and couldn't wait to get home.

GROWING PAINS AND APOLOGIES

At sixteen, I was doing my best to fit into a busy, blended family, but while I wasn't aware of it at the time, I had become a walking apology. Whether it was Saturday chores or other tasks of the day, I just couldn't live up to Stacy's expectations and had made a habit of apologizing for my shortcomings.

"You didn't fold the towels properly," she'd say. Sorry. "That pot's not clean. You need to wash it again." Sorry. "You didn't wipe the table down well enough, there's still crumbs." Sorry.

Sorry. Sorry. Sorry.

If Walter was around, he'd sometimes vouch for me. "Well, I don't know," he'd say. "The table looks fine to me."

"You're just not looking at it in the light," she'd say, then angle her head. "I can see bits. Don't you see them?"

Not wanting to press the subject any further, Walter would shrug and shuffle away in the moccasins he liked to wear at home.

At the time, news sources were abuzz with the political tensions of the Cold War, but like many of the other kids at school, I was more interested in the impending launch of the space shuttle *Challenger* and the female crew members aboard. Months later, most of the developed world would watch as history blew up into tragedy, live on television, when the shuttle exploded and all seven crew members died.

Walter did his part to educate us kids about the world. "Yep, a push of a button and the world as we know it could be over," he'd say. But I didn't want to think about things like that. The family had already seen the movie *Threads* a few years earlier about the impact of nuclear war, and that had been enough for me. But the filming of George Orwell's novel *Nineteen Eighty-Four* in 1984 caused another buzz in our house.

"You heard of it?" Walter said. "You should read it."

While I was too immature to think that Orwell's notions of Big

Brother and the Thought Police could ever exist, Walter believed that kind of technological world wasn't too far off. "About twenty years from now," he said, "there'll be technology that will be able to track people. They'll be able to put a computer chip in people's wrists. Not only that, but you'll be able to talk to people on the computer and see them on the screen." But it was hard for me to believe at the time that technology could be taken so far.

One evening Stacy arrived home from work with the Intellivision video games *Donkey Kong* and *Astrosmash*.

"Why did you buy video games?" Walter asked.

"I didn't," she replied. "They came with the computer I purchased for the office."

I didn't find these games engaging. I preferred to play my flute or read. I'd recently become aware of the legendary author Charles Dickens, as Walter owned *The Complete Works*, the thin, Bible-like pages bound between thick, burgundy hard covers. It was important, he told me, to understand the common theme to be found throughout Dickens's works, that of the disparity between the classes. The family had seen the filmed version of *A Christmas Carol* quite a few times, and in the last few years it had become a tradition to fill the living room with the Ghosts of Christmas Past, Present and Yet to Come every December 24. To this day, Ebenezer Scrooge's transformation and his role in saving Tiny Tim still brings tears to my eyes and fills me with hope. We'd seen *Oliver Twist* as well, the story of the orphan whose life struggles weren't helped by Bill Sikes and Fagin, but like me, Walter found the books to be better than the movies. In the evenings he liked to read in the living room, sitting in the beautifully handcrafted wooden rocking chair he and Stacy had recently purchased. "It will look great in the log house," he said of that chair.

The boys were becoming quite the mischief-makers now that they were getting older and more agile, and when they climbed onto the rocking chair, I worried it would flip right over and send them flying. One morning Tony sent the house into a panic when we couldn't find him, and it turned out that he had walked right out the front door. Fortunately the kindly neighbour who had taken him in heard me frantically calling his name as I stood in my housecoat in the middle of the road. After that, Walter installed a deadbolt at the top of the door so Tony couldn't escape and scare the living daylights out of us again. But another morning I discovered him on his bed unsuccessfully cracking eggs into a mixing bowl, while Theo, held hostage in his crib, had smashed eggs and processed cheese slices all over his sheets.

When I asked Tony what they were doing, he said cheerily, very pleased with his cleverness, "We're making pancakes!"

"That's great," I replied, "but let's clean up and make them in the kitchen, okay?"

The worst of their mischief was when Ron and I had to spend hours cleaning up the mixture of shit and diaper cream they had spread all over the textured walls of their bedroom. It must have been a Saturday because Stacy added this disgusting task to our chore list. To put an end to their cooking adventures, Walter tied the fridge door shut with bungee cords and locked the freezer downstairs too, tired of disappearing ice cream. Whenever he wanted some, there'd be only the slightest skiff at the bottom of the pail. "Who ate all the ice cream?" he'd bellow. Ron, Pat and I knew who was guilty, but we never said anything as Walter always said, "Nobody likes a tattletale."

Locks didn't resolve little Theo's problems as he woke whimpering in the wee hours practically every morning. Walter and Stacy apparently believed in the "crying it out" theory. Not wanting to step on their toes—particularly Stacy, who would send me dirty looks when the boys came to me for cuddles if they bumped their heads or had a fall—I'd listen for a good five or ten minutes in case his parents wanted to wake and deal with him. It was only when nothing happened that I'd carry him to my room, and I can't remember how many times I felt a warm, damp sensation along my thigh as he slept beside me, the cuddly little brat. Luckily the disposable diapers he wore at night were more absorbent than his daytime cloth ones, so my lovely new bed wasn't ruined.

Although that bed was new to me, it wasn't really new. Walter had arranged for me to buy it for only a hundred dollars from one of his colleagues, whose daughter was grown and no longer needed it, and he said that once I was ready to leave home, I could take it with me. It wasn't the canopy bed I had dreamed of when I was younger and was really too old for now, but a twin bed with a creamy headboard decorated with fancy gold trim and a matching dresser with a mirror attached.

"Phyllis," Stacy said one evening, "I have someone from work coming for a dinner meeting tomorrow. I need you to make something nice." She must have thought I was a good cook by then, as I prepared the family's meals so regularly. My secret ingredient was mushroom soup, which was really Stacy's secret ingredient because I used her recipe book, the one she had been using for years to make quick, easy-to-prepare meals. It wasn't long before I could make some of them by heart: mushroom soup mixed with rice and meatballs, mushroom soup mixed with onions to bake pork chops, and mushroom soup mixed with tuna, onions and noodles. To add variety, I'd make the odd meal of macaroni mixed with cheese, tomatoes and ground beef, and there was always my picnic special of beans, wieners and pineapple. Everyone in the family seemed to enjoy these meals as they all ate heartily, and even the boys enjoyed their mashed-up version, Tony sitting at the table in his booster and Theo in his high chair.

While I was a bit shaken by Stacy's demand on this occasion, I said, "Sour cream chicken?" This was a family favourite.

"Yeah, that would be great. I need it ready for five o'clock."

The next day the nanny reported that the boys had a good nap, so while I prepared dinner, they were happy to play in their room and hone their dress-up skills. Clothes were everywhere as they pulled items out of the lower drawers, and every once in a while I'd peek in and encourage them. "You look great. How clever you are getting dressed all by yourself," I'd say, and they'd smile broadly. At one point Tony had his pants on backwards and Theo had his brother's training underpants placed crookedly on his head like a hat.

Once I had the chicken roasting nicely in its sauce, I took the opportunity to help them clean up the mess and then tempted them with a dinner of cheese and crackers. By the time Stacy arrived home, they were happily fed, the rice was cooking and the broccoli was gently steaming.

"How's the dinner coming?" she asked, marching into the kitchen, donning the mitts I'd put on the counter and opening the oven door to check on the entree.

"Good," I answered, standing by her as she slid the casserole dish toward her to get a closer look.

"Did you remember to take the giblets out?"

"Giblets?"

"Yeah, giblets," she countered, as if I should have learned what they were by osmosis. "Don't you know what giblets are? Whenever you have a whole chicken, you have to take the giblets out!"

Taking my confused look as a no, she turned my beautiful caramel-coloured chicken over carefully while I watched in dismay, worried it would fall apart. "It's all right. There aren't any," she said, while I breathed a sigh of relief that my chicken still looked okay. "Now quick, I need you to take the boys downstairs and keep them quiet! This is a really important meeting!"

Within moments of gathering the boys and closing the rec room door, I heard the doorbell ring and Stacy welcoming her guest. A couple of hours later, having entertained the boys with nursery rhymes, toy cars and books, I settled them into bed and left them softly singing. I was heading back downstairs, not wanting to interrupt the "important meeting," when Stacy called me into the dining room. She and a gentleman with a moustache and spectacles were sitting at the table with empty plates.

"This is Robert," she said.

"Hi. It's nice to meet you," I said, nodding.

"I really enjoyed the dinner. You're quite a cook," he said kindly.

"Thank you," I replied awkwardly while Stacy grinned proudly. I should have taken her silent pride as my compliment. Instead, I hung around thinking she might actually compliment me with words, but then she turned to Robert and began, "Hey, I have an idea ..." So I continued on my way downstairs. My favourite sitcom, *Family Ties*, starring that teen heartthrob Michael J. Fox, was coming on.

—∞—

One day my friend Ursula dropped by unexpectedly. She had moved into a rundown house a few blocks away, a six. Like me, she moved frequently as her parents also chased cheap rent. At school I'd often share my lunch with her; she seldom packed one because she was ashamed of her mother's thickly sliced homemade bread. We'd each have half of my sandwich, bites of one apple and one cookie. I would have liked to offer her more, but Stacy had strict rules about how much lunch I could take.

When I told Helen of Ursula's problem, she sent extra, which helped even if it was only one day a week. She knew Ursula was my best friend and had even invited her on the odd Wednesday for a sleepover. We had whispered and giggled until well after bedtime, and Helen eventually had to ask us to be quiet.

When Ursula arrived on this day, I was in the middle of preparing a tuna casserole. "You cook for them too? Isn't it enough that you already take care of their kids and do most of the housework? Can't you see they're using you?"

"It's not so bad," I replied with a shrug, changing the subject to school. But the truth was that I kind of liked cooking, and the boys were cute, greeting me with a hug when I came home from school every day. When it came to Saturday chores, if Stacy was at the office, our tasks were more fun and passed by more quickly because we could turn up the stereo to the tunes of the Police or Tears for Fears. Even Stacy liked to turn up the stereo in the evenings if she was in the mood, usually after a couple of drinks, grooving to seventies hits, doing the Beatles head shake and encouraging all of us to dance with her. We older kids would join in, holding the boys' hands as they wiggled their little hips, while Walter sat on the couch, laughing at the performance.

Besides, just as Walter had said years earlier, things could be worse. At least Ron and I were together and we lived with family. What would have happened to us if Walter and Stacy hadn't taken us in? I was certainly better off than poor Shelly Wheeler at school. Ursula told me how she'd been bounced from foster home to foster home because her mother had died and her father couldn't cope. She was a heavyset, unkempt girl who looked tough, walked tough and talked tough. While I didn't realize it then, just under that tough veneer was a bubbling anxiety that would boil over into a raging temper when unkind teenagers, usually boys, called her names. Once they got the results they wanted—her face turning bright red, her yelling and spewing all sorts of obscenities their way—they'd laugh and sometimes taunt her even more before they wandered off, still laughing.

I think caring and compassionate Ursula was Shelly's only friend. While I never befriended Shelly because her unpredictable moods scared me, I never made fun of her either and would smile shyly at her in the halls. But even after moving in with a loving, supportive family who attended Ursula's church, losing weight and adopting a completely new look, Shelly just couldn't get a break, and the taunting continued. There was no way my life was even close to being as hard as hers.

Not that my life was dreamy. There was no time for dreaming, not even when we headed off for "holiday time" at Walter and Stacy's log home, because there were endless jobs and constant problems to resolve there. The pump would need priming, the generator would break down, the radio phone wouldn't work, the pipes would freeze, the chimney needed cleaning, wood required chopping, meals had to be prepared, the boys needed tending and more. Fortunately most of the maintenance of the equipment that kept "the cabin" functioning fell to Walter, but of course Ron, Pat and I all had to pitch in.

I was usually in charge of the boys on these holidays. One late spring evening, after I'd spent a dull day indoors with them, I was looking for some excitement, so after putting them to bed, I got permission to walk to the holiday cabin of the Davis family across the river. On occasion we'd played cards with them, gone swimming or chatted round a campfire together. I put on a light jacket and headed into the black, moonless night, making sure to take a flashlight. When I got to the rope bridge Walter had built across the river at the far end of the meadow, I looped the handle of the torch around my wrist so it wouldn't accidentally fall into the water and carefully placed each step.

It wasn't until I was walking up the hill on the other side and heard coyotes yipping in the distance that it occurred to me how crazy I was to be alone in the dark forest. Remembering Walter saying that animals don't like surprises, I started singing John Denver's "Leaving on a Jet Plane," picking up my pace at the same time. It wasn't long before I saw the light of the Davis cabin ahead, a welcome beacon. A few more minutes, I thought, and I'll be safe inside their cozy cabin. When I knocked on the door, Mrs. Davis welcomed me but looked over my head, searching for the rest of my family.

"It's just me," I said.

"We were just getting ready for bed," she said. "I'll drive you home."

I had practically risked my life looking for some fun, and it had all been for nothing.

—◊—

Walter must have felt the pressure of the numerous tasks waiting for him every time we went to the cabin, and there were times when his natural sunny warmth turned cool, like the time I had been in charge of housework and the boys for what seemed like days. We'd just had a pancake breakfast that he prepared on the new log-fed cooking range while Stacy, in her housecoat, had looked on, jogging on the spot in an attempt to lose her "baby weight."

"Why do I have to stay inside and take care of the boys all the time?" I asked, while Stacy tried to figure out the workings of the new oven. "Can't someone else do it?"

"Sure," Walter answered. "You and Ron can trade jobs. He can watch the boys and you can chop wood."

Well, let's just say that didn't go so well, not on my end anyway. I didn't weigh much more than a hundred pounds at the time, and after I'd made numerous attempts to split one piece of wood, tears of frustration flowed down my cheeks. Walter's reaction was not what I'd expected. Sitting on a nearby stump, he said sarcastically, "What? Can't you do it? What's so hard about splitting wood? You're the one who didn't want to watch the boys."

Another time I pushed him to his limits when I complained just loud enough for him to hear, "All we ever seem to do is work. We never have fun anymore." As I began sweeping the plywood floor yet again, he surprised me by grabbing me from behind and throwing me to the floor. As he straddled me I could see the frustration in his eyes, and I wondered fearfully what he'd do next.

"Shut up!" he yelled.

Fortunately Ron hadn't ventured outside to chop wood yet, and he told Walter firmly to get off me. And he did.

━━

The summer of 1986, Ron and I were hired as sheep drivers for one of Stacy's make-work projects, aimed at reducing the invasive fireweed that was overtaking the local native plants. Because we were working in the middle of dense forest, we'd buy food in town for the week and then bunk in campers. As I was the only girl among the half-dozen workers in the crew, not to mention the youngest, Ron and I shared quarters. During the day we took turns tending to the animals, alternating in two-hour shifts.

On our "on" shifts, sweaty and uncomfortable under the sun beating down, we drove the herd of a few hundred animals along the dusty roads, making sure there were no strays, while they ate their way through the brush. At times one of us would raise the alarm when sheep would wander off, and we'd have to guide them back to the flock. During our "off" shifts, we were free to do what we liked, though our options were limited, considering our remote location. I liked to cool off in a nearby creek, then sunbathe on the bank and either read or practise flute.

Before nightfall we'd drive the herd back to home base, where we'd gather them into a corralled meadow, though this could be tricky at times because sheep can be really stubborn. Luckily the manager owned a border collie. We'd tell her to "go around" and she'd nip at their heels to get them where we wanted. Good girl!

After a hearty dinner followed by card games, we'd settle for the night, though there were times when we had to reach for our flashlights before dawn because the sheep had broken out of their corral, fearful of predators. We'd round them up and repair the fence, making plenty of noise to scare away any lurking wolves or cougars. After a while, we learned to keep a ghetto blaster belting out tunes through the night to scare away predators, the noise muffled by the camper walls so we could get some sleep.

The only sheep I remember losing that summer was a worn-out ewe. After we had corralled the herd one evening, I spotted her nearly lifeless body lying in the middle of the gravel road, and I pleaded with Ron to save her.

"Maybe she's overheated," I said. "Maybe she just needs water. Can't you carry her to that puddle?"

"She's dying, Phyllis," he said. "It won't make any difference."

"Please, Ron, please," I begged, feeling so bad for her. Eventually he lifted her heavy, smelly, rag-doll body to the nearby puddle, where I willed her to drink, hoping she'd survive. But as we prepared for the drive the next morning, there she was, dead in the middle of the cloudy puddle where we'd left her.

We worked only alternate weeks as sheep drivers but still got full pay because we were on call 24-7. I made sure to save as much of my pay as I could, as I was determined to go to university. Edward and Helen were encouraging my plan to become a teacher. "Music would make a great specialty for you," they said. Ron, meanwhile, was considering communications, as he had been stage-managing school plays and volunteering at the local cable station.

⸻

When we saw Mom later that summer for our semi-annual visit, I didn't mention that I had spent the previous eight weeks working out in the bush with a bunch of young men. I didn't think she'd be pleased, even though Ron had been there with me. Instead, as we were old enough now to venture out without her, we shared the excitement of Expo 86, the huge transportation and communications exposition that Vancouver hosted that summer. Pat joined us too. Mom's place was crowded with the five of us, but she made it work.

With the birth of the SkyTrain a few months earlier, it was a fast and easy trip from Mom's place in New Westminster to Vancouver, which, being on global display for Expo, had been cleared of all the unfortunate homeless. I took pictures of Ron and Pat perched on steel transportation structures and various motorcycles and cars, and standing among crowds of people as world flags flapped in the gentle wind and Science World shone in the background.

One afternoon Mom had fun wandering around Expo with me while the boys enjoyed rides like the roller coaster and the log flume. In one picture that I took, she's wearing slacks and a matching blue blouse, her hands crossed in front of her, smiling. That was the day she had decided to quit smoking "cold turkey," because Ron and I had been nagging her for the last couple of years. "It isn't good for your health," we said, "let alone your pocketbook." After a few hours without a smoke, there she was in the middle of the busy fairground, taking a puff on the largest cigarette I'd ever seen, but barely able to hold it as her hands were shaking so much.

"Mom! What are you doing? What the heck is that? I thought you were going to quit!"

"It's a cigar that Roger gave me. I'm sorry, Phyllis! I just can't do it."

I realized then how addicted she was. She was having, as she liked to call it, "a nic fit."

"It's okay, Mom. Don't worry about it," I said, before we went on a desperate search for somewhere to purchase cigarettes.

I was glad that she and I were able to work through the slight disagreement we'd had the evening before. After a long, fun-filled day, on the way back to her place, we kids had got separated among the masses of people. Ron and Pat were able to make it onto the SkyTrain, but the doors closed, "ding, ding, ding," before I could join them, and we looked helplessly at each other through the window as the train departed. I caught the next train a few minutes later. Although I was a little worried being on my own, I was more worried for Ron and Pat, as I knew Mom would be pissed they'd left me behind.

When I arrived at her apartment building close to an hour later and walked down the hall, even though I hadn't heard her raised voice in years, I recognized her screeching yells. "HOW COULD YOU LEAVE HER THERE? NOTHING BETTER HAPPEN TO HER!" And as I entered the room, she turned on me too. "WHAT THE HELL DO YOU THINK YOU'RE DOING WORRYING ME TO DEATH?"

I knew she was anxious about my safety, but it wasn't exactly the welcome I needed. I didn't mean to miss the train. I turned on my heel and walked right back out the door, settling under the weeping willow in the park. Taking in the quiet evening, I sat on the cool grass, gazing at the twinkling red and white lights of the cars crossing the Pattullo Bridge and listening to the traffic hum and the occasional honk echoing in the night.

A little later I heard her calling, "Phyllis? Phyllis?"

"I'm here, Mom, under the tree."

"Oh, thank goodness. I'm sorry. I didn't mean to yell. I was just worried."

"I know, Mom. I know," I said, standing up to face her.

She wrapped her arms around me then in a gentle embrace, and I rested my head on her shoulder.

"Come on inside now, okay?"

"Okay," I replied as she took my hand, and we walked back to her apartment together.

To this day I can still feel her soft, silky skin, her warm palm wrapped in mine.

SUITCASES

My last year of high school got off to a poor start. Ursula's parents had split up, and she had left town with her mom. I hung out with Michelle instead. While I don't think I had been aware of it at the time, I had appreciated that my lost friend had accepted me the way I was, unlike Michelle, who figured I needed advice to fit in at school. But I took her guidance, as she was outgoing and confident. She suggested I wear baggy shirts to hide my shapeless figure, and I began wearing my thrift shop jeans with the oversized U2 T-shirt Ron had given me. She showed me how to swagger—strut, wiggle, strut—and how to stand in line with one knee bent and a hand on my waist. "It looks better," she'd say.

Michelle lived a few miles south of town in a plain-looking rancher, which on its own would have been only a seven, but as it was nestled in a picturesque valley surrounded by evergreens, with a rustic barn beyond providing the perfect Cariboo scene, I'd say it was an eight. Her plump mother, Patty, raised horses, and her wiry father, Daniel, was a handyman.

I had joined a group of girls at their house for movie-night sleepovers a few times over the previous years when Walter and Stacy hadn't needed me to babysit. While her parents watched a show in their bedroom, we girls would watch chick flicks in the main room, but I usually fell asleep, which created a good laugh. As I was dozing off, I'd hear, "There goes Phyllis, falling asleep again." I seemed to have a gift of making people laugh, not with me but at me. One lunch hour I was sitting next to Michelle in the cafeteria when somebody asked if anyone had seen the Lamborghini in town.

Naively I inquired, "What's a Lamborghini?"

"You don't know what a Lamborghini is?" Chuckling laughter.

Stacy laughed at me too when she thought I should know something I didn't, but what I remember most is her condescending tone.

"Oh my gosh, you don't know that?" At least Michelle never laughed at me.

I was happy that Walter and Stacy sometimes allowed Michelle to come to the house after extracurricular activities at school to wait until her father finished work in town. "As long as she doesn't interfere with your chores," they said. She would help me entertain the boys and prepare dinner.

One evening she said, "You sure do lots of work for your aunt and uncle. You cook their meals, watch their kids and tidy their house. Don't you think there's something wrong with that?"

With Michelle telling me the same thing Ursula had told me just months earlier, the following Saturday when the same chore ritual took place, I spoke up. Stacy had just placed the list on the table when I asked, "Why do we always have to do all the housework? Why don't you ever help?"

"I have other things to do! I'm busy!"

"Too busy to clean your own house?"

"You can't speak to me that way! Wait until Walter gets home! Do your chores *now!*"

"WHY SHOULD I?" I shouted back, losing my cool, leaving her rolling her eyes as I stomped to my room and slammed the door. *Wham!*

Moments later Ron gently opened the door and sat next to me on the bed. "Why did you have to talk to her that way? Why can't you just do as she asks?"

"Because it's true, Ron. She should help out. Don't you think so?"

"Well, it may be true, but I find it's best to keep her happy. The way I handle her is I just do what she says. It works. She likes me."

"Easy for you to say. She hates me," I replied, thinking that she only ever talked to me when she wanted something.

"She does seem to like me more, but who can blame her?" he said with a huge grin.

"Funny," I answered, appreciating his humour and playfully punching him in the shoulder, my simmering temper calming, before giving in to the Saturday ritual.

When Walter got home later that afternoon, I got a lecture. "Stacy tells me you were rude to her today."

"Yeah, a bit, I guess," I answered sheepishly, "but I just suggested she help with chores, that's all."

"You're missing the point, Phyllis. You can't speak to Stacy that way. You're grounded for a week."

—∞—

Fortunately I wasn't grounded when the opportunity arose for me to play first flute in the provincial high school honour band at the University of British Columbia in Vancouver. While I was performing pieces such as "Send in the Clowns" and "Rhapsody in Blue" in that huge auditorium, it was nice to see Mom and Roger standing at the back while Granddad and Joan sat among the crowd. Walter must have told them about it. My aunt and uncle had come to my first festival performance back when I was twelve, but since then they had attended only a couple of school concerts. Whenever I performed in music festivals, recitals and award ceremonies, I'd look into those audiences of proud parents knowing that none of them had come to hear me play. This time, when the music ended, I was the one beaming proudly when my mother and grandparents told me how much they'd enjoyed the performance.

I wish I still had the taped recording all the musicians were given. It would have been great to relive the experience of that amazing symphony. I'd even been selected to play a duet. The dozen or so flutists in the orchestra had each given a brief audition before the director, and afterwards he had pointed his baton at me and another girl. "You and you," he said. What a thrill! At the time I thought I'd safely stowed the keepsake cassette in my top drawer, but a few months later I discovered I was wrong.

While I thought it was unusual that Aggie, the boys' nanny, hadn't greeted me after school and I instead found Stacy on the couch doing paperwork while the boys played in their room, I continued down the hall to find my door open. When I crossed the threshold, I couldn't believe the sight. My room was a shambles. Clothing was hanging out my drawers, and other belongings were scattered all over, including my UBC cassette. The magnetic ribbon was pulled out, torn in sections, and strewn across the floor.

I walked quickly back down the hall to the living room. "Stacy, what happened to my room?"

"It's not my fault," she said defensively. "The boys did it. I was working!"

"But … but …" I knew that if I blew a fuse and let out my frustrations, I would be grounded. Instead I returned to my room and did my best to tidy up. My clothes were easy enough to fold again, but my precious cassette wasn't such an easy fix. I sat on the floor, trying to rewind the delicate tape with a pen and using Scotch tape to splice the torn pieces together. I thought that if the boys had destroyed her room on my watch, I probably would have been grounded for a month.

After dinner I asked Walter to help repair the tape, as he could fix practically anything, but it wasn't long before he admitted there wasn't much he could do with it. Reluctantly I placed my treasured cassette in the trash. I wish now that I had had the sense to ask for another copy or perhaps make a copy from one of my bandmates' cassettes, but all I have today of that amazing experience is a faint memory.

I figured the ordeal was over, but the next evening Walter and Stacy summoned me to the main room, which they did only when there was more work to do or if there was trouble.

"The boys found this in your room yesterday," Walter said, holding up a note. It took me a few moments to realize that it was a letter from Michelle, describing her mixed feelings about an intimate encounter with a boy a couple of years earlier. I'd forgotten I even had it, but I found it hard to believe they had read my private letter.

"Are you seeing a boy?" Stacy asked.

I was quick to answer, "No!"

Not anymore. They knew I'd gone out with Jerry, a soft-spoken boy from school, a quiet kid like me. Our relationship, which went as far as holding hands, had lasted only a few short weeks. We broke up after he'd invited me to his house one evening, and Walter and Stacy had allowed me to go after I told them what he had told me: that his mother would be there. She wasn't. Jerry had lied. While he showed me around the house, I felt nervous, worried about his intentions. Upon opening the door to the master bedroom, he pushed me onto the bed, then jumped me, and I pushed him off, yelling, "Stop!"

"You don't want to make out?" he asked.

"I just want to go home." He was kind enough to accompany me down the empty, dimly lit street, while we talked awkwardly about the constellations in the black sky above us. I spent the following days avoiding him. When he showed up at the house several days later with a gold chain for me, I refused his gift and told him I didn't want to be a couple anymore.

"Well, we hope not," Walter said now. "We don't want you to end up pregnant. It would ruin your plans for university."

"When I had Pat," Stacy added, "the nurses treated me like dirt because Walter and I weren't married. We don't want the same thing to happen to you."

"No, really, I'm not seeing anyone," I reassured them. "Can I have my note back?"

Walter placed the letter in my hand, and I returned to my room, thinking that at least they were looking out for my future. I may have been a victim of a sly and cunning man, Edward, but I was nothing like them. They didn't really know *me* at all.

——∞—

Over dinner one evening late that fall, Stacy suggested we spend Christmas at the new log house. We older kids exchanged glances with the same question: How would we get there through all the snow? But Walter and Stacy hadn't purchased a new four-by-four extended-cab pickup for nothing. We would load it with supplies, skis and toboggans and end the last days of 1986 in a wintry expedition.

It took two days to get us all to the cabin. The first morning of the trip, when it became obvious that the truck was spinning its wheels too often, Walter cut the engine miles before we arrived at the one-lane bridge, leaving the vehicle right in the middle of the road, not worried about blocking anyone's way since we were miles from civilization. The road, narrowed by snowdrifts, was unrecognizable, and the forest on either side was as colourless as a black and white photo.

We older kids were happy to stretch, having travelled more than an hour with our knees around our ears. Ron was now given the difficult task of breaking trail to the cabin on skis, followed by Pat and me. Walter was next in the procession, pulling the toboggan of food, including the Christmas feast, while Stacy brought up the rear, pulling the bundled-up boys on a sleigh. With only backpacks to contend with, Ron, Pat and I were able to ski faster, and we arrived at the cabin within a few hours and got the fire going. Walter arrived without his sled just before dusk, having left the food buried in the snow. Stacy had turned around and taken the boys home again because the task of pulling them was taking longer than expected and daylight was waning. Instead, we all met up early the next morning where Walter had left the food buried, and this time, with Ron in charge of the Christmas feast, Walter led the way, pulling the boys on the sleigh. With the trail already broken, Walter was well out of sight when Ron lost control of his loaded toboggan as he inched it along a ridged embankment, dumping most of the food supplies, which rolled to the bottom of the hill. Seeing the toboggan keeling to one side, Pat and I had yelled at him to watch out, but we were too late.

"You guys get down there and pick all that up!" Stacy ordered.

After taking off our skis, we scrambled down the hillside, sinking in the snow up to our knees. Fortunately the heavier items, such as the frozen turkey, had stayed on the crest of the hill, but the canned stuff was hidden at the bottom in icy tunnels. Stacy helped by standing on the trail and pointing them out. "I see another one! Look there, under that tree! And there's another to the right!"

After a week of cabin coziness interspersed with chores, tobogganing and skiing, on the day we returned home Walter and Stacy gave Ron and me our Christmas presents: one large and sturdy canvas suitcase each.

———

The snow had melted and the grass had turned brilliant green when Mom caught me off guard one day by calling the house, something she never did. When Walter handed me the phone, she told me worriedly, "I have breast cancer, Phyllis." All I remember saying lamely was "That's terrible! I'm sorry to hear that." I know now she was looking to me for support, but I was too young to understand that at the time. Needless to say, I spent the coming days filled with worry for her.

When I told Walter the bad news, he said there was a good chance she could recover if they had caught it early enough. Helen, being a nurse, said the same thing, that there had been medical breakthroughs. And so did David, the new social worker I saw monthly, which was more often than I'd seen any other social worker I can remember. His office was conveniently located on my walk home from school, and our appointments were usually brief and cheerful. "I guess I'm a pretty easy case, eh?" I commented at one point. "You must have way more challenging cases out there." And he agreed.

With all this reassurance around me, I tried to be hopeful about Mom. I told myself that Granny's cancer had gone into remission, and maybe Mom's would do the same. But then, with my mother occupying so much of my thoughts, I began to worry that I would develop schizophrenia too. *This is why I'm so naive that people laugh at me*, I thought. *This is why good grades don't come easily to me.* In spite of my best efforts—studying during lunch hours and between chores and amid the family hubbub—I just couldn't reach the B honour-roll standard that I'd managed in previous years. With the exception of music, my grades had dropped to average. On top of that, I was failing algebra and had signed up for an English literature correspondence course a couple of months earlier to make up the necessary credits so I could still graduate. But even with Edward's help, I could barely comprehend the material, all the thees and thous in Old English. When Stacy asked about my progress, not to upset her, I lied and told her I was further along than I really was. But somehow she found out, and once more I was grounded. "Why am I the only one who ever gets grounded?" I shouted, my voice gradually getting louder and more agitated. "It's not fair. It's not fair! IT'S NOT FAIR!" More stomping followed by another slammed door.

I knew the school had called numerous times to report that Pat had skipped classes, yet he was never grounded. When Ron punched a hole in the wall, frustrated because he wasn't allowed to go to a party, he wasn't grounded. If anything, he was liberated. He had just turned nineteen. After fixing the wall, he was allowed to take the truck practically every weekend. I'd hear teens at school saying, "Did you hear that Ron got so drunk at the party last Saturday that he passed out in a ditch?"

I was the responsible one. I never skipped classes. I never partied. I didn't want to drink like Aunt Stacy and I didn't want to smoke like my mother, who had been telling Ron and me for years, "Never start smoking, because once you start, it's hard to quit." Walter, feeling nostalgic after our trip east, had told me about the time his teenaged brother Jack had crawled up the driveway one morning, high after a night of partying. "He was never the same after that." With Helen and Edward constantly reminding me of the effects of alcohol and marijuana on the brain, I didn't even smoke the dope the teens passed around the smoke pit that I walked by every day. "Did you know that every time a person gets drunk," Helen said, "they lose thousands of brain cells? Marijuana's just as bad or worse."

At my next appointment with David, I told him I felt treated unfairly. He suggested that I tell my aunt and uncle, but hadn't I already done that? I didn't tell him that Stacy just rolled her eyes when I was upset. I didn't tell him that she had never thanked me for all the chores I'd done. It was not that I expected a thank you all the time, but some appreciation once in a while would have been nice. At least Walter thanked me on occasion. When I did up the buttons on the dress shirts I'd laundered so they'd hang nicely, he said, "Thanks for washing my shirts, Phyllis, but can you not do up all the buttons next time?"

My meeting with David ended with my gravest concerns. "What if I turn out like my mother? What if I develop schizophrenia?" If that happened, I wondered if I'd end up poor like her, too, unable to hold down a job, all my hopes and dreams dashed.

"Just because your mother has schizophrenia doesn't mean you'll get it." His words helped a little, but my worries lingered for years.

——⚬——

Later that spring I was able to put my worries aside at the BC Festival of the Arts on Vancouver Island, competing on the recommendation of the festival adjudicator. Even though I didn't win, I had a great time and heard many talented musicians. Unfortunately, to avoid falling behind at school, I returned earlier than the other local musicians and missed my connecting flight at the daunting Vancouver airport. My heart fell when I asked a service worker why my plane hadn't arrived, and she told me it was long gone and I'd have to settle for the next flight a few hours later. I figured I had been too immersed in my book to hear my flight announcement.

I hated to tell Stacy. When she picked me up, she shook her head. "It was just too much for you, wasn't it? Too difficult for you to catch the right flight." I did my best to ignore her comment while I fetched my Christmas suitcase from the luggage rack.

As we headed home listening to tunes on the radio, I couldn't help but think that if Helen had attended, as she had the previous year as a member of the festival committee, there was no way I would have missed my flight, and all of this wouldn't have happened. But Helen had a lot on her mind these days. Both she and Edward did. For months they'd been coping with allegations of abuse by one of Edward's students. They had tried to hide their troubles from me behind their rigid smiles, but I heard their strained, whispered discussions when they thought I was sleeping. I could feel the looming question that hovered over them like a dark cloud: *What are we going to do?* The allegations had spread through town like wildfire, diminishing them to shadows of the loving, happy couple I'd first met, and as Edward's reputation faltered, his school's population dwindled, and long friendships ended.

I was filled with anxiety for weeks, wondering if there would be a trial and if I'd be called to testify. I had already decided to say that Edward was a man of fine character, not wanting to draw attention to myself or further wound Helen. They had done so much for me: giving me free music lessons, driving me to other cities to take exams and paying for them too. (I discovered only a year before writing these pages that it was about this time that Walter and Stacy had started paying for my musical tutoring, and I recalled Stacy asking me to find out how much Helen charged her flute students.)

When Stacy heard about the abuse allegations, she suggested that perhaps my music lessons should stop. "There's no way I'm giving up my lessons!" I said, and she heeded my objections. She knew how much Wednesdays meant to me. A few months earlier, after the dentist had told her I needed skin grafting for gum recession, I'd run to my room, worried that this operation would not only dampen my rich woodwind tone but prevent me from producing any sound at all, and she had surprised me with the one and only display of sympathy toward me that I remember. "You'll still be able to play the flute, Phyllis," she had assured me gently. "I'm sure it won't make any difference." I wasn't going to risk losing my favourite day of the week. And with Helen now working day shifts, Edward hadn't come for me in months.

It was a good thing my lessons continued because Ron and I were graduating from high school, and Helen was making my prom dress. The school halls had been filled with excited chatter for months. "My mom's taking me to the city next week to buy my dress," one of the girls said. "I think I'm going to go with soft pink. Do you think the colour will suit me, or should I go with pale blue?'

I didn't carry around the excitement the others did. I told myself I didn't care about the dinner and dance, I didn't care that nobody had asked me to be their date, but I knew that I didn't really want to go because I didn't have proud parents eager to spend time there with me. When I told Walter and Stacy that parents were invited and asked if they wanted to go, Walter had laughed. "Why would you want us there?"

If it hadn't been for Helen, I wouldn't have even gone to the prom. She was the one who told me, "It's an important time in your life," and she insisted I should ask Stacy about buying me a dress. As I was responsible for buying my own clothes now, I wasn't surprised when Stacy said she couldn't afford one. When I told Helen her answer, Helen said, her lips tight, "Then we'll make one."

I wish now I'd been more appreciative of her efforts, the hours she spent working with the slippery, silky fabric she'd bought in Victoria. I helped here and there, but I was hopeless at sewing and I wasn't really interested. In fact, I don't really remember my prom at all. Ron, who attended with a pretty date on his arm, told me Walter and Stacy did come for the grad dinner of Chinese food. Earlier that afternoon, after presenting a deserving student with a bursary from the bank, Walter had stayed just long enough to see Ron and me walk across the stage before heading back to work, but he had returned later with Stacy for the dinner reception.

I was truly surprised, however, to see Ursula as the grads mingled later with the proud audience. We shared hugs and teary laughter. "You look great! How've you been? So wonderful to see you!" She didn't stay long, but she sent me the pictures she took, which are still in my album today, among the few I have of the momentous occasion. In one of the pictures I am standing on the school field by the parking lot in my unbecoming coral dress with its sweetheart waist and puffed sleeves.

With high school over, I was set to start my summer job as a cashier at the local hardware store in a few days, the job Walter and Stacy had encouraged me to apply for. "Have you dropped off your resumé yet?" I didn't have the same motivation to find a job that Ron did, but he didn't have much choice. Since he'd turned nineteen, with government cheques no longer arriving for his upkeep, he'd been holding down two restaurant jobs to cover his $300 room and board with Walter and Stacy.

To celebrate the end of school, Michelle and I made plans to go camping for the weekend, just the two of us, at Emerald Lake, but when I asked Walter and Stacy if I could go, they said they needed me to babysit. Michelle couldn't believe it. "You what? You have to watch their kids on grad weekend? Have they ever paid you for all the babysitting you've done? You should just come anyway."

"I don't think that would go over very well."

"Aw, come on, Phyllis. What's the worst that could happen?"

I thought about this and decided I could live with grounding, which I figured would be my punishment. So on Friday evening, I packed what I needed, placed a note on the coffee table explaining that I'd return in a couple of days, coolly walked past my aunt and uncle as they sat reading on the couch and then continued across the street to where Michelle was sitting at the wheel of her parents' silver Granada.

We were heading to the lake in the morning, and she talked excitedly about the camping trip. Even though I was excited too, a small part of me had a feeling of foreboding. Sure enough, shortly after we'd settled in her living room to watch a movie with her father, Walter showed up in the van.

"You need to come home," he said, as we stood in the kitchen where I'd gone to talk with him. Although Daniel had answered the door, he had ducked back into the living room to allow us privacy. "If you don't come with me right now," Walter added, his eyes boring into me, "I'll call the police."

I stood my ground. Looking straight into his intense, troubled eyes, I said in as strong a voice as I could muster, "Call them." He bowed his head, left the house and drove off.

The police never came, though I told Daniel I was worried they might. As he sat in his recliner nursing a cup of coffee, with Michelle listening, I filled him in on the recent happenings. He shook his head in disbelief, reassuring me that I hadn't done anything wrong.

"I don't know what I'm going to do now," I said. "How can I ever go back?" I knew that soon Ron wouldn't be around for moral support, as he had announced a couple of weeks earlier that he'd be moving in with a soccer mate, Mike, and his family. His room and board would be a hundred dollars cheaper there than what he'd been paying Walter and Stacy.

Michelle piped up, "Can she live with us?"

Turning to me with a smile and a wink, Daniel went into the adjoining bedroom to talk to his wife, gently closing the door. He returned moments later and said kindly, "You can stay, Phyllis."

"Really? Are you sure?" I asked, while he nodded.

Michelle's eyes widened and she hugged me. "We'll be like sisters!"

I was too filled with emotion at her family's kindness to say anything, but I think Daniel saw my glistening tears of thanks.

The next evening, after setting up our tent by the lakeshore, Michelle and I talked in the warm glow of our campfire, watching the sparks fly and listening to the wood crackle. Or, rather, she talked while I listened. Like many of our classmates, she had already been accepted to a university and planned to move in the fall to the Lower Mainland, where she would live with her grandparents. "It's going to be so much fun, Phyllis! I'll be able to hang out with my cousins."

I wasn't going anywhere soon. I had been looking forward to living near Mom, but all my university applications had been rejected. I don't know why I had thought I was university material when I wasn't, not with borderline grades and a failing grade in algebra. In fact, I wasn't sure what I was going to do. Helen and Edward were encouraging me to go back to high school to upgrade and then apply for college, which would "probably make an easier transition" to university. But I hadn't found a place to stay anyway. I'd asked Granddad and Joan if I could stay with them in their three-bedroom condo, but they said they needed the space for an office, and Mom said her place was too small, that there'd be nowhere for me to study, which was true.

When I think of it now, I realize the enormity of my question to my mother, asking to stay with her when she was so ill. A couple of months later I'd see the effects of the cancer myself—all her beautiful hair gone and the nausea she was experiencing. But she put on a brave face, apparently more worried about her looks than her ailment. "How do I look as a blond, Phyllis? There were only a few free wigs to choose from." Later, after she'd had a mastectomy and her luscious hair had grown back, she again asked how she looked, as she stood in her casual outfit wearing the special bra underneath her blouse.

"You look fine, Mom," I would say. "No one can tell."

Meanwhile, back at Michelle's place on that fateful day, I placed a clipped call to Walter, telling him that I'd be moving out and would come by in a couple of days to pick up my belongings. When Michelle and I arrived that pleasant Sunday afternoon, Ron had just placed his Christmas suitcase filled with his clothes in the back of his friend's truck, parked behind Walter's shiny pickup. As the driveway was crowded with the Jimmy and van parked there as well, Michelle parked her parents' boat of a car on the roadside in front of the house.

Walter and Stacy had packed up my belongings for me. My Christmas suitcase filled with clothes was on the lawn, ready to go, along with the rest of my belongings stuffed into black plastic garbage bags. Michelle helped me carry them to the car. The only thing that was missing was my lovely bedroom set, so I went to open the front door to arrange to pick it up, but the door was locked. I knocked.

"You don't live here anymore," Stacy said icily upon opening the door. "You're not welcome."

"But my bed. You said I could have it," I replied.

"That's true," Ron piped up from where he stood on the driveway. "You did say she could have her bedroom set when she moved out."

By this time Walter had come down to the landing. "Shut up, Ron. This has nothing to do with you," he said coldly, then turned his attention back to me. "You don't live here anymore, Phyllis. You're not welcome." And he closed the door.

I was too upset to speak, but I'd feel bad later that I hadn't said goodbye to the boys. What a surprise Pat would come home to, I thought. He knew Ron would be leaving, but he had no idea I'd be gone too. Ron and I looked at each other for a few moments, stunned, then he shrugged. What could we do? We gave each other a hug, wished each other luck and exchanged contact information.

As Michelle drove us to her place, my tears poured. "I don't understand why they're being so mean. I'm a good person, aren't I? What have I done to be treated this way?"

Michelle was dumbfounded, as were her parents. "It's not you, Phyllis," they said.

When I told David my side of the story, he arranged to meet with Daniel and Patty, and after they passed a criminal record check, it was agreed that I could stay with them. To encourage my coming independence, as I was just seventeen, not yet the age of majority, I would receive the monthly government cheque of $260 directly, paying $200 for room and board to Patty. Michelle had kindly offered to share her room and had cleared some of her drawers and shelves.

On a sunny afternoon while Michelle and her parents were tending their horses, I tackled the task of sorting my belongings, which had been haphazardly packed without any care. Buried beneath the clothes in one of the garbage bags, I discovered the *Watch Me Grow* book I'd received back in 1979. Abandoning the task of organizing my belongings, I pulled it out. It had grown thicker over the years. Opening the faux leather binder, I gingerly flipped through the pages of my life.

It was only in the last couple of years that I'd filed away some of the early records that Mom had somehow managed to save from our house fire. She had given them to Ron and me, saying, "You're old enough now to have this stuff." As I sorted through them, I found my baptismal certificate and a hospital wristband from when I'd had tonsillitis when I was too young to remember. I found early report cards and faded class pictures from when we lived in the city. I looked into the smiling faces of friends, playmates and teachers I'd left behind: Miss Brown, Laura, Annie, Rani, Ricky, Jeff and other classmates whose names I can't remember. My first crush in grade one. Keith? The boy who looked up the skirt of the cute choir teacher, who was too immersed in song to notice. I came across swimming badges from the days of Bonsor Park and other class reports and souvenirs my mother had lovingly kept through the years.

As I turned the remaining leaves, I found five pages with the same heading: My Foster Family. I'd already filled in the first page with the names of my brother, aunt, uncle and cousins. I flipped to the second page, then found a pen. Beside My Mother, I wrote "Patty." Beside My Father, I wrote "Daniel." Beside My Sisters, I wrote "Michelle." Then I placed the book on the shelf, finished unpacking and headed out to the barn.

Michelle was exercising her horse in the corral. She steered the coffee-coloured stallion to the fence and asked if I wanted a ride. "No, thanks." I was no longer a fan of horses. Besides, I felt safer where I was. I needed to feel the firm ground beneath me. While Michelle returned the stallion to his stall, I watched the sun setting behind the hill, the dark blue sky lit up with hues of yellow and pink. Then I turned to face my new home and walked toward the rest of my life as if I knew which path to follow.

Part Four

BLIND FAITH

I was moving forward, one step at a time. At my summer job I took to my cashier training like a duck to water, speedily counting back change and whipping through long lineups of customers, making sure to take advantage of my employee discount by stashing away Christmas gifts: a set of towels for Mom, a desk lamp for Ron and a scarf for Roger. I even purchased a set of casserole dishes for Walter and Stacy, hoping we'd be over our differences by the holidays. I was disappointed that I hadn't heard from them on my birthday, but my spirits lifted when Daniel and Patty surprised me with a cake.

Helen and Edward remembered my birthday too. Having kept up my weekly lessons, I still saw them regularly and was happy that they were slowly recovering now that the abuse allegations had been proven untrue. While they were dealing with the allegations, their beloved spaniels had died, but they had adopted a boisterous, bouncy pup, which gave them both some new, positive energy. Shortly before they presented me with my gift of a *Pocket Oxford English Dictionary*, I had taken their advice and returned to high school, hoping to move to the Coast when the term was done to attend college. Unfortunately my post-secondary plans would fall through yet again, because the semesters didn't line up. With only a few days with Ron, Mom and Roger during the festive season, without Michelle's company and with very little work besides the odd babysitting job or shift at the video store, I spent most of that long winter lonely and depressed. It didn't help that my hope of reconnecting with Walter and the family was waning, as I still had heard nothing from them.

My uncle finally called in March. Having heard from Ron that I was basically unemployed, he asked if I would stay at the log house for a week while the family was away. He would pay me a few hundred dollars. Eager to put our differences behind us and have my family back, I agreed to take up his offer. On a frigid afternoon a week later, Walter and I addressed each other coolly at the highway junction where Daniel dropped me off. There must have been a lighter snowfall that year because I don't recall any snowpack, but I remember that the land was frozen. As we drove along the narrow gravel roads, we made small talk that continued through the family dinner and into the morning, putting the past behind us with nobody mentioning the dramatic weekend I'd left home.

What I enjoyed most was seeing the boys again. Theo had lost his toddler looks and Tony sounded so much older with his expanded vocabulary. They were shy at first, but it wasn't long before they were holding my hands and sitting in my lap while their parents prepared for the journey. Pat and I were able to catch up too, and I laughed when he told me he'd had a beer on the plane when he and the boys had gone to spend the summer with Granny, a reward he had given himself for taking on the responsibility of toting two preschoolers through the massive Toronto airport where they'd changed flights.

"Really? A beer?" I said. "But you were only thirteen!"

Once the family had gone, I passed the time reading novels by the wood stove, walking in the frosty meadow and practising flute.

⸺

"There's something I need to tell you." Edward's tone was sombre. It was a fine spring morning, and we were headed to town to pick up his few remaining students. I could tell he meant business, so I caught his eye in the driver's mirror. "Remember back when we met?" he said. "I'd gone to your uncle that day to ask to adopt you, but he said he wanted to keep you and your brother together and in the family, so that's when I came up with the idea of Helen teaching you flute." He paused for a few moments while I took in his words. "I'm not going to live long, Phyllis. If something happens to me, can you promise that you'll take care of Helen?"

"But I won't need to, Edward," I answered, uncomfortable with his words. "You're not going to die!"

"Just promise me," he repeated.

Thinking there was no need to make such a pledge to the man I'd endured for years, I nodded. I'd do anything for Helen, the woman I adored who had been withering away during the previous year as she stood faithfully by her man.

———

With summer tourist season approaching, I was happy to be earning again, waiting tables at a popular restaurant in town. I worked the lunch shift, which I preferred, as did my manager because the busy dinner hour left me flustered and I muddled up orders. Ron, having completed his first year of communications studies at Capilano College in North Vancouver, had returned to take on a summer job of tree planting, and he would often come by after a long day on the job for a slice of strawberry cheesecake and a large milk. A fellow he knew from the cable station had kindly lent him his 1970s van, so when I saw this psychedelic-looking vehicle approaching, I'd have his snack on the table waiting for him before he could sit down, and if business was slow, I'd take my quarter-hour break with him.

We shared our mutual relief after he spent an afternoon with Mom listening to records and was able to tell me that her latest cancer checkup had come back clear. "And I saw Walter the other day," Ron said. "He says you're probably never going to leave this dead-end town and you're going to be stuck here forever working in a dead-end job."

"Let him think what he wants," I answered. "I've already been accepted by Cap College."

After his congratulations, we made plans to room together at the Coast. When the cool fall breeze was creeping into the late summer air, Ron finished his last week of tree planting while I headed for the Coast to stay with Mom and look for a suitable rental in North Vancouver. I remember sitting at her kitchen table, checking the classifieds and announcing my findings to her. She'd make comments like "That place sounds good" or "Seems expensive." Eventually I saw an ad for a two-bedroom apartment and made plans to take a look. Roger kindly offered to come with me.

With its new carpeting and north-facing balcony overlooking a wooded park, it looked good, and it was an easy walk to various shops and a simple trek to the bus to the college. After telling Ron about the place, I met with the landlord, who was delighted to have a brother-and-sister set of college kids as tenants; we filled out the paperwork and didn't have to look any further.

Friends donated mattresses for us to use as beds, we purchased a used couch I found advertised in the paper, Joan was happy to pass on a Formica dining table with a set of dishes, and somehow we inherited a free-standing television. The picture was crooked and we had to fiddle with the antenna to get good reception, but it worked. For the finishing touch I purchased some potted plants, and our home was born.

When we showed Mom around a few days later, she said the place was "real nice." We knew she was happy to have us less than an hour away from her apartment in New Westminster. Granny had written, "I hope you visit your mum quite often—she's so happy to have you so close." Later that week the excitement continued when Ron surprised me with a dozen red roses and treated me to a coming-of-age dinner in a fancy observatory restaurant with spectacular views of the city, sea and mountains. We enjoyed fine food and shared laughter and good times.

Unfortunately, within days all that warmth evaporated. When I came home at dusk after a long day of classes, I found Ron slouched in a chair, holding his head in his hands. Dropping my backpack of books, I asked, "What's wrong?"

He looked up at me. "Someone called about an hour ago. She said her name, but I can't remember it. Edward passed away this morning. Heart attack. I'm sorry, Phyllis."

I stood speechless for a few moments, then turned away and walked to my room. As I lay on my pale blue comforter staring at the ceiling, I thought back to the day Edward had told me he didn't have long to live, and I hadn't believed him. *How could he have known?* Now I was filled with mixed emotions. I didn't know whether to cry or feel relief, assured by the knowledge he'd never bother me again. Eventually my thoughts turned to lovely, kind-hearted Helen. After all she'd been through, I was worried how she would deal with more anguish. That's when I was able to cry, but my tears were for her.

As soon as I was able to get away, I went to visit her. When she met me at the train station, I saw how her overwhelming grief had aged her by at least ten years; she was gaunt, pale and so fragile that she looked as if a wind or harsh word could knock her over, but stoically she held herself together. When we arrived at her home, she seemed more concerned with my needs than her own.

"We'll sit by the fire. Would you like some tea?"

"That would be great," I answered, reaching to put the kettle on, but she stopped me, insisting on doing it herself.

"I've lost my husband, Phyllis. I'm not disabled. It's good for me to keep busy. I'm going back to work next week. I've already had a week off, and that's long enough. I can't stay here wallowing in sorrow. I need a distraction. I know people will talk, but this is how I want to deal with things. Everyone has their own way of grieving, and this is mine. Thank goodness I work days now. I don't know what I would have done with Tippy if I still worked nights."

"Sure, Helen," I said. "Let them talk. You have to do what's best for you."

While we sipped our tea, and Edward's favourite chair sat empty, she told me about the service. "He'd like the place he's resting, Phyllis, beneath a lovely cedar tree." I agreed, saying that it sounded beautiful. If she thought it was odd that I didn't offer to see his final resting place, she never mentioned it.

Over the next couple of days, I took some solace in knowing that at least Tippy, who was nearly a year old by that time, had become her loving and trusted companion. He followed her everywhere, lying by her chair while she read, trailing behind her to the kitchen, then to her bedroom. He'd bark at the door if she left him inside while she gathered firewood, and he'd come obediently when she called him back from forays to chase squirrels or an animal scent into the forest. She used the same call that she had for her cocker spaniels, her singsong voice echoing the notes mi-do through the trees.

That last day in the Cariboo, I found it hard to leave her and wished that I'd stayed with her rather than visiting with Daniel and Patty, to whom I felt indebted because they'd been so good to me. As she and I stood in their driveway in a parting embrace, I was the one who was now overwhelmed with grief. Daniel had to gently prod my arms off her. Then she turned quickly toward her car without so much as a backward glance, likely to escape my distressing sobs as I watched her go, worried how she would manage alone.

Weeks later she sent me a letter saying that while she appreciated concerned visitors dropping by, she was grateful for private time, too, which gave her a chance to remember how special Edward had been. She went on to say how busy she was dealing with the extra tasks he'd always done, like car maintenance, stacking wood for the furnace and doing all the paperwork. She ended her letter with the hope that I was studying hard. "My love till next time and regards to Ron. Tippy sends a lick and a wag!" It was the first of many letters we would exchange. She remained a mother figure to me as the years passed and in time would become like a grandmother to my daughters.

I was studying hard at college. Once I got used to the coastal rain again and learned to carry my umbrella everywhere, using the work ethic and time management skills I'd developed balancing toddlers and chores with school and music, I settled into a disciplined routine. But while I took my college classes seriously on weekdays, pouring myself into my studies, on weekends I allowed myself a break, and that's when Ron introduced me to the Vancouver nightclub scene. We'd lose ourselves in the crowd on the dance floor of Luv-A-Fair, our bodies moving robotically in the dim shadows and flashing lights to the music of offbeat alternative bands like the Cure and Skinny Puppy. Other weekends I'd meet up with Michelle, who was working for a security company in Burnaby after deciding that university wasn't for her. We'd groove among a different crowd to upbeat top-forty tunes. On these nights, I'd treat myself to one drink, a rum and Coke, the drink I'd discovered when Ron took me out for my birthday dinner, then I'd sip water the rest of the night. I was there for the dance release, not the booze.

Besides, I had to watch my spending. Even though I'd received student loans and the grant money Helen and Edward had encouraged me to apply for, and Ron had worked out in the bush each summer, the two of us were just scraping by, surviving on cheap student fare of pasta and potatoes. We appreciated the times Granddad and Joan took us out for a three-course meal. We'd tell them about our classes, and Granddad would talk about his Masonic conventions and their important fundraisers. "You know those buses around the city that transport disabled children? We paid for those," he informed us. He was very proud that we were both attending college. "Knowledge is power," he'd say. On one occasion he added, "My mother was a teacher, you know."

We appreciated Mom's home cooking too. She couldn't afford to take us out for a meal, but she made a mean cheese sandwich, then we'd run errands together or walk through a city park if the day was clear. Once, as she, Roger and I strolled along the Beaver Lake Trail in Stanley

Park, we had stopped to admire the reflective water when I spotted one of the elusive animals the trail is named for. "Over there! Over there! See it swimming?" I yelled excitedly, pointing, until they saw it too.

Even with all my frugality, it wasn't long before I realized that I needed a job if I was going to stay in college. I didn't want to cash the savings bonds Granny had given Ron and me to help with college, as I figured we should let them collect interest. As I had experience waiting tables, one grey misty day I took my resumé to a popular restaurant franchise, figuring the tips would be good, but within moments of walking through the door, I knew I'd never be hired. The busy waitresses had chic hairdos, impeccably applied makeup, fashionable high heels and stylish black outfits. I felt like a country bumpkin in my outdated, threadbare winter coat, scuffed flats and makeup-free skin. The manager barely looked at me when I handed him my resumé; he would call if he needed me, he said. He never called.

I didn't get the next job either, even though I was better prepared. When I dropped off my application at this popular steak house, I made sure to look as sharp as I could, though the best I could do was my high school concert band attire of black skirt and white blouse. I primped my hair, buffed my flats, highlighted my eyes with mascara and traded my old winter coat for a polyester blazer. I was shivering, but I looked good. Before long, I was called for an interview, and it went really well. When the manager called days later, I was expecting to be hired, but instead she asked me to come for a second interview. By then I was running out of clothes, so I traded my skirt for dress slacks, which still looked smart with my blouse and flats, but then I botched my chances by telling the truth when she asked if I liked steak. Red meat, I answered innocently, wasn't really my thing. That was the end of that.

Fortunately my boyfriend, Tyler, came to my rescue. I can't recall the exact moment we met, so it wasn't love at first sight, but I do recall that we were in the same history class. One morning shortly after the term had started, he had recognized me at the college bus stop and offered me a ride in his shiny blue Volkswagen. We'd been dating ever since. He lived with his mother in a quaint house not far from the college, and she would invite me for dinner from time to time and always sent me home with leftovers.

Tyler was just as generous. One fall afternoon we ventured inside an expensive boutique, where he suggested that I try on some of the coats. They were well out of my price range, but when a quilted lavender coat seemed to be made for me, he bought it for me. Really? Thank you! Thank you! I had never realized how wonderful an item of clothing could make me feel. I strutted out of the store. I strutted on the sidewalk. I strutted onto the bus, willing people to look at me in my beautiful coat.

His generosity continued when he helped me land a job. When I told him my predicament, he said that the five-star restaurant where he worked was looking for bussers. "You have experience, right? I'll put in a good word for you." I dropped off my resumé, which the staff had a good laugh about later, calling me Little Bo-Peep because of my sheep-herding days, and I was hired part-time.

The place was just as fancy as the one Ron had taken me to for my birthday. Tyler told me that one of the waiters had been an English teacher, but he quit teaching because, with all his tips, he earned more money as a server. For a brief moment I questioned my own career choice, but then I remembered how scattered I became when working the busy dinner hour in my last restaurant job. Besides, it soon became apparent that I didn't have the personality to wait tables for the rest of my days. On one particularly busy Sunday buffet shift, an expensively dressed lady with greying hair and a large diamond on her hand beckoned me over. When I asked politely if she'd like anything, she replied rudely, eyeing her empty dish with disgust, "Would you *please* remove my plate?" I was so taken aback by the way she spoke to me that I answered, "Certainly," then walked away, busying myself with other tables and leaving her with the offending item. All I could think was she had no right to speak to me that way! Some minutes later I returned, smiled and removed her dish.

I worked there throughout the summer of 1989. By then I had successfully completed my first year at Cap College, but I knew I would have to get more hours at the restaurant to continue. That's when the head chef, Stephan, kindly offered me the position of prep cook. He gave me a tour of the kitchen and explained my duties, and I accepted the job without fully understanding what I was getting myself into. I don't think he understood what he was getting into either, as he soon realized how hopeless I was. I chopped the vegetables too slowly. I whipped the cream too much. I served the portions too small. I soaked the pasta too long. And then there were the demands of the servers. Where's number four? I asked for seafood, not steak! How long is that soup going to be? It was all I could do to hold back tears as I ran around among all the shouting, barely able keep my thoughts straight.

—∞—

In the meantime Ron was looking ahead to his graduation when Granny suggested he complete his final practicum in Ottawa. "That way you could meet your dad," she said. On our next visit with Mom, when we told her Ron would be meeting our father, she said, "I bet he hasn't changed at all. Probably still likes his booze."

Later, as we walked to catch the bus, Ron turned to me. "What do you think? Should I meet him?"

"What could it hurt? Once you meet him, you'll find out how you feel."

When Ron returned two weeks later, he told me he had not only met our father but that Sherry, our blond aunt "with the fancy house and pool," had hosted a family gathering where he met almost our entire paternal line. Our father, he said, was "actually really nice. He bought a round for everyone at the pub. Everyone there knew him!"

Mom's comment when Ron showed her the pictures he had taken of our dad with an ever-present pint of beer in hand was "Still drinking, eh? He hasn't changed a bit."

—∞—

While Ron and I had been busy pursuing our education dreams, Walter and Stacy's Cariboo dreams had become harsh reality. After their cattle-raising operation failed, they ventured into sheep farming, and when that had not proven viable either, Stacy had taken a job in the Fraser Valley, creating government work programs as she had done in the past, coming home only on weekends. Walter must have missed adult company because in the early spring he called me to ask what I thought about Mom visiting him at the log house, and I said she would probably love it, which she did. While I was on the phone with Walter, I asked after the boys, and he told me they were doing well in their correspondence lessons.

"But Theo's only four. Isn't he too young to start school?"

"If I'm teaching one of them, might as well teach them both."

"You mean to tell me they're in the same grade? Do you think that's good for Tony's self-esteem?"

"What's the big deal? He doesn't care."

"Maybe not now," I answered, "but don't you think he will when he's older?"

"It'll be fine," he assured me.

I knew there would be no changing his mind, so I let the subject drop. A few years earlier, he hadn't listened to my opinion about Tony's left-handedness either. "He'll have an easier time in life if he's right-handed," he said. "They don't make anything for lefties." And he forced him to use his right hand.

About the time Ron and I were ending our college terms, Walter and Stacy were ending their Cariboo dream. They sold the sheep, locked up their log home and moved back to the Coast, where they settled temporarily in a suburban rental. I felt badly for Walter at the time, but over the next few years he and Stacy transferred their dream to a new location, buying a stunning house on acreage in the Fraser Valley and covering the land with sheep, a couple of workhorses and a vegetable garden. They sold their Cariboo home and the beautiful property around it and used the profit to pay off the mortgage on their new venture. I still cherish my memories of the rolling hills and endless meadows of my Cariboo years, particularly the earliest days there, when my life was still fresh and more carefree.

Meanwhile, one fine afternoon shortly after Walter, Stacy and the boys had moved to the rental house in the Vancouver suburbs, I had called and arranged to drop by for a visit. I dressed in a lavender peasant skirt from the thrift shop with a lacy top I'd recently purchased. With months of regular earnings, I was slowly trading my frumpy wardrobe for new items like streamlined skirts, skinny jeans and fitted tops, though I always bought on sale, feeling liberated by not having to buy thrift.

After a brief hello to Walter, who was tidying the kitchen, I wandered into the living room to greet Stacy, who was telling a long-time friend from the insurance agency about her new sports car. But most of my visit was spent reconnecting with the boys and chasing them around an adventure playground in the nearby park. Before I left, Walter asked if I'd like to have the boys visit with me for a few days, the beginning of a pattern that continued throughout their school years. A week or so later he brought them by with sleeping bags. The following morning we made pancakes, and later I took them to the park down the street. I had just finished pushing them on the swings and was heading to a bench to sit down when, to my horror, Tony, without a care in the world, pulled down his pants and peed right in the middle of the play area. Living in the bush hadn't given him any inhibitions. I pretended he wasn't with me and looked the other way. When Walter came to pick them up, he found my ordeal hilarious, and he was still chuckling when he asked if I wanted their double bed as they'd acquired a new queen-sized one, perhaps his belated amends for denying me the bed I'd purchased years earlier.

Only weeks later Mom and I celebrated her birthday together, spending a glorious day at a public market and then enjoying a birthday dessert at the apartment I shared with Ron. Instead of cake, I had concocted an ice cream pyramid topped with caramel, nuts and chocolate chips. When I retrieved this special surprise from the freezer, she exclaimed, "Wow! That looks good," and we enjoyed every sugary bite, digging in with two spoons.

By the time the festive season came around, since Walter and Stacy as well as Granddad and Joan were busy with their own plans, Ron and I invited Mom and Roger to spend Christmas with us. Our apartment was roomier than Mom's bachelor pad, and with my new bed, they could comfortably spend the night with us. I didn't mind sleeping on the couch. Mom and Roger arrived Christmas afternoon, carrying an overnight case, a bag filled with colourful packages and her miniature silver tree to put them under. Oh, what a lovely time we had! Mom and I decorated the tree with shiny baubles, placing an angel on the top and arranging our few meagre presents underneath, while the guys talked about pop bands. Afterwards I talked about college while Mom helped me in the kitchen, taking over the cooking of the turkey that Ron and I had purchased earlier at the supermarket up the hill. (I was relieved that the heavy plastic bags full of groceries hadn't given way as we carried them the ten or so blocks back to our apartment.) Once I'd filled the bird with Stacy's famous sausage stuffing, I began sealing it up, following the directions Joan had given me earlier over the phone.

"That's not how you do it, Phyllis!" Mom exclaimed.

"Well, I don't know! I've never done this before!"

"Well, just move over. Let me do it! You're supposed to lift up the legs like this, then tie them together, see?"

Instead, I busied myself preparing the vegetables, impressing Mom with the quick chopping technique I'd finally mastered as a prep cook. Once the turkey was carved, we made a toast "to family" with sparkling apple juice and enjoyed a fine dinner. I was especially proud of the cranberry sauce Tyler's mother had told me how to prepare, just by following the instructions on the package of berries.

When we retired to the living room with full bellies, I was pleased that Mom liked her gift. She was always so hard to buy for. She never gave me or Ron a sense that she wanted or needed anything. Fortunately, I had found a reasonably priced book on the royal family. She was delighted, laughing with glee as she flipped through the pages and admired the pictures, particularly those of her beloved Princess Di. Afterwards I poured more sparkling juice, then put on the pop tape *A Very Special Christmas*, and Roger persuaded Mom to dance. How sweet they were swaying to "The Little Drummer Boy" and other festive tunes, their arms round each other, while Ron and I relaxed on the couch and flipped through the royal book, savouring chocolates.

That "very special Christmas" of 1989 would prove to be the last days in years of recovery for my mother, the last days her brain was well enough to manage her life, the last Christmas our little family would ever celebrate together. She had survived cancer, but she wouldn't survive a relapse triggered by a letter she was about to receive.

As a twenty-year-old college kid, I did my best, but without understanding her illness, I didn't have the power to help her. I missed the signs, such as her change in appearance and the strange stories she told. When I did glimpse her need for help and reached out, there was nobody to tell me what to do. As a result, my mother got sicker, so that at last the symptoms that had been slowly hijacking her thinking pulled her footing from under her and caused her to stumble on the cracks within a faulty system where all that was there to catch her were bullets.

INVISIBLE WALLS

Ri-i-ing, ri-i-ing! Bells bringing in the festive new year?

"Hello?" I answered, picking up the phone.

"Phyllis?"

"Hi, Mom," I replied, hearing the worry in her voice.

"I just got a letter in the mail. They're going to tear down my building," she said in practically a wail. "There's asbestos in the walls. I have to be out of here in three months!"

"Gosh, Mom, that's horrible."

"What am I going to do?"

"We'll figure something out."

"Can I move in with you guys?"

A pause. More ringing bells, an alarm for the freedom I thought I'd lose. All I pictured was my mother telling me what I could or couldn't do, and I didn't need that, not after living under the rules my aunt and uncle had imposed. All I could think was that living with my mother would be going backwards.

"Why don't I help you find your own place instead?" I asked, thinking that the social worker she'd mentioned on occasion could likely help as well. "That would probably work out better."

She'd found other places to live, I told myself, my mind filing back to the places we'd lived in Burnaby. I didn't know then that my grandmother had found those places. When she had visited from Ottawa all those years ago, she had actually come to find Mom a home and had stayed for a week to do it. I had always thought it was odd that she'd come such a long way only to see her grandchildren for an afternoon.

"Okay," she said hesitantly before hanging up.

Meanwhile, in between classes and assignments, Tyler, in his naturally generous way, offered to take Mom and me to the addresses I circled in the paper. While I don't recall my mother's monthly rental budget, it must not have been more than a few hundred dollars, $400 at most.

The first place we checked out was a one-bedroom basement suite. While the landlord—an older gentleman—showed us around making idle chit-chat, and Tyler mentioned we were in college, Mom followed, nodding from time to time and saying things like "It's all right" or "Mm-hmm." And we added comments like "The living room is large" or "There's plenty of natural light."

The owner seemed keen, though not for long. "So, when were you saying you needed the place for?"

"Oh, any time soon, but the place isn't for me," I replied innocently. "It's for my mother."

Until that moment I hadn't thought how peculiar she looked—her lack of facial expression, her sometimes calculating stare, her withdrawn manner, her old-fashioned thickly framed glasses and her slow-moving gait as she walked around in her sixties throwback camel coat. To me, that's the way she was; that's the way she had always been. She was my mother.

The fellow didn't know what to say and tripped over his words, no longer looking me in the eye. "Um, well … I'll have to think about it."

Tyler told him we had another place to check out anyway, so we thanked him and headed off to the next one. We got the same response there. The owner was kind and chatty until he found out the place was for my mother, not for us.

"It's because I'm on welfare, isn't it?" Mom said accusingly.

I'm ashamed to say that I was embarrassed by her tone, so I quickly intervened. "It's okay, Mom. There are other places."

Sure, there were other places, but not for her. Over the next couple of months, we got the same response everywhere we went. Nobody called back, and when we called, they said the place was no longer available. Perhaps it wouldn't have made much difference, but I never thought to ask for a reference letter from her apartment manager. As far as I knew, she'd always paid her rent on time. She would skip meals before she'd skip rent.

The three months were nearly up when she called to say she had found a place and invited Ron and me over to see it. So, on a warm afternoon in early April, we went to the address she had given us, a cement tower located in the midst of a concrete jungle at a noisy intersection, a far cry from the quiet neighbourhood she had left a few miles away. What I remember most is the confusion that ensued before we even entered. There was a cluttered keypad outside the lobby door with various tenant names and presumably their apartment numbers beside them, but there seemed to be no logical order. And Mom's name wasn't there. We figured that, as she'd just moved in, her name hadn't been added yet, but when I pushed the number she had given me, somebody else answered. I apologized for the mix-up.

"Maybe you accidentally pressed the wrong button. Let me try," Ron suggested.

I assured him I hadn't pressed the wrong one, but he tried anyway. The same person answered and we apologized again.

"Maybe Mom got the numbers mixed up or I wrote them down wrong," I said. "Maybe it's 301, not 310. Try that."

Nope. More apologies.

We stood looking at the jumbled mass of buttons, names and numbers for a few moments, wondering what to do. That's when Ron freaked out on the busy sidewalk.

"What the fuck!" he yelled. "This is ridiculous. We came all the way out here and now we can't even see her!"

"Would you calm down? You're not helping! We have to think! There's a pay phone down the street. We'll call her." No such thing as cellphones then.

"Yeah, good idea," Ron agreed calmly.

"Mom? We're here, but we can't get into the building. Yes, I know you gave me your apartment number. Can you come to the lobby and meet us?"

"The intercom's not working properly?" she inquired when she came out to look a few minutes later. She stood staring at it, shook her head, then led us into the elevator and up to her bachelor pad. The place seemed nice enough, a little larger than her last, and she had her furniture neatly arranged, though I never thought to ask how she had moved it all. While Ron and I commented on the city view and the wood floors, enjoying the glasses of water she'd poured for us, I was suddenly aware of the noise from the neighbouring apartment, somebody's hacking cough over a television program. I don't know why it never occurred to me at the time that I wouldn't have wanted to live in a place where the walls were so thin that I could hear my neighbour coughing. My only explanation is that my ignorant, selfish young self was just relieved Mom had found her own place. On top of that, I realize now that Roger wasn't around. I hadn't seen him since Christmas, and Mom hadn't mentioned him lately either. I'd learn later that he'd bailed out, confused by the changes in Mom's behaviour. But at the time I didn't see it as a sign that anything was wrong.

A week later she wasn't answering her phone, which was not like her. When Tyler called me, I told him how odd it was that she hadn't picked up, and he suggested we check in on her. Ron came with us. This time, even though the intercom was still a jumbled mess, we figured out the proper button to push, but there was no answer.

Now Ron and I were really worried. Tyler took control and called the manager, explaining the situation. Moments later, a fellow about my mother's age opened the lobby door, unlocked her apartment and then left. Mom was sleeping, or so I thought before we noticed the half-empty pill bottle on her bedside table. Oh. My. God.

"We have to wake her up!" Tyler said. "I'll call 911!"

In the meantime Ron paced while I shook her by the shoulders. "Mom, Mom, wake up!" I don't know if I even believed in God, but I began begging him to save my mother. *Please, God, please, God, let her be okay.*

Groggily she lifted her head and mumbled something incoherently. Yes! She was conscious!

Just minutes later two paramedics arrived. Tyler hadn't thought to mention on the phone that my mother had schizophrenia. While I didn't know this at the time, if he had, the police would likely have come as well, just as they had when Mom was a teen. Decades later my uncle Walter's words when I was a schoolgirl in the Cariboo would echo in my head—"Whenever she went into hospital, the police, the paramedics, they were all men"—and I'd realize my young uncle had witnessed this same traumatic situation on more than one occasion. Later, in my twenties, he'd refer to the stress that permeated his childhood home. "I couldn't move out fast enough. Granny and Granddad didn't see eye to eye when it came to your mother. They argued a lot."

Although that had been over fifty years ago, to this day, rather than mental health professionals attending a mental health crisis, "usually the police are the first responders," I was told by the facilitator of the mental health workshop I took in June 2015. "It's not ideal," she said, "but that's the way it is for now."

Turns out the police had to be called anyway. My mom was that sick. Moments after the paramedics entered the room, she somehow staggered to her feet, walked to the kitchen as if in a trance and opened a drawer. When it dawned on me what she was doing, I pulled the large knife from her hands as she raised it to strike. The paramedics thanked me and then apologized because, now that she had drawn a weapon, they had to call the cops. "Just do what you have to do," I said. Anything, I thought. Just save my mother.

While we waited for the police to arrive, we all stood speechless, our eyes fixed on the woman who stood in the middle of the room like a statue, her arms folded across her chest. I didn't even recognize her. And just as I didn't understand what was happening long ago when my brother and I went into foster care, I didn't understand what was happening now.

Minutes later two policemen arrived in full gear, their guns holstered at their hips. It was hard to watch as she allowed them to handcuff her and then lead her to the elevator. Ron accompanied her to the hospital while Tyler and I followed in his car.

All I remember of that day after that is standing in the hospital corridor and Tyler telling me, "They made her drink charcoal so the drugs are out of her system. They'll keep her here for a while. She's going to be all right. We can go home."

With finals looming and Mom in the hospital, I attempted to study, but it didn't seem to matter how many times I read the textbooks, I couldn't focus. The words on the page were mixed with the repeated question in my head: *What the heck is going on with Mom?* Realizing that I was overwhelmed, I decided to drop a class and reached for the phone.

A few days later I sat across a tidy desk from the college's dean.

"What can I do for you?" he asked.

I didn't quite know how to frame my request. Finally I said, "Well, I, um, my mother, she, uh, tried to … commit suicide and I … well … want to drop my orchestra class."

"Why? There's not even a final."

No words of empathy. No offers of support.

I couldn't look at him. Instead, I looked down at the pink capris

I was wearing and fumbled with my fingers. I knew what I wanted to say, but the words wouldn't come out because my throat was so tight. I couldn't tell him that I knew there was no final, and that's why I'd chosen the class. I didn't need the credits for my university transfer.

A teardrop.

"Fine. You can withdraw, but I still don't understand why."

I thanked him, overly thanked him, in fact. Now, all I can think is *What a fucking jerk.*

A few days later Mom called to tell me she was out of hospital.

"So you're feeling better then?" I asked.

"I'm doing all right."

She wasn't, but I wanted to believe her.

Ron and I had discussed why Mom had tried to take her life, and we figured she hadn't really wanted to die; she just wanted attention, though we never thought to ask her. As far as we knew, she had never tried to kill herself before. But she had. Twice. When we'd first moved west. Relocation and a failed marriage are hard on anyone, let alone someone with poor coping skills. As far as I can tell from her records, with too many changes for her brain to manage, she had gone off her medication. Then, with anosognosia and hallucinations setting in, she had attempted to take her life. On one of those occasions, she was sent home from emergency within hours of swallowing charcoal, but my grandmother advocated for my mother by appealing to her psychiatrist. He had arranged to have her admitted, and she spent weeks in the hospital attending social groups and life skills classes to make sure she was well into recovery before being released again.

This time, a couple of weeks after Mom's release from hospital, I phoned her to arrange for an outing to Shannon Falls with Tyler. While I had her on the line, I told her that with my second year of college behind me, I had been accepted to university. She was really happy for me and also pleased when I told her that, at Helen's suggestion, I was considering volunteer work with children so I could apply for the teaching program. "There's a community centre down the street that runs child care programs."

A couple of days later we set off for Shannon Falls, and after admiring the scenery along the way, my mother laughed when the light mist of the waterfall sprayed our faces, and she continued to laugh right through our alfresco lunch. I thought, *How wonderful that she's relaxed and enjoying herself.*

Not too many weeks later Granny and her new husband arrived in town. She had met him on the bus while en route to visit her sisters in Manitoba a few weeks after Dennis, her second husband, had passed away. This new husband was a kind, soft-spoken fellow who wore polyester shirts, plaid slacks and loafers. They spent most of their time at Walter and Stacy's, but they did take us grandchildren to Science World. I remember Granny and I discussing how Mom was doing and agreeing that she would report her thoughts to me on that subject after she had spent an afternoon with her. Her conclusion was that Mom was doing fine.

"Really? Are you sure?"

"Yes. Really. We had a lovely lunch, then we took her shopping. We told her she could have anything she wanted, and she chose a simple cotton dress. She was thrilled. You know your mother. She's always been easy to please."

With Granny's reassuring words, I cast my worries about my mother aside.

—⚬—

By then I'd been working for a time as a server at a Chinese restaurant. This scruffy place was a far cry from the posh dining room where I had worked across town. This one even had the odd cockroach scurrying across the counter, not to mention fruit flies, but at least I didn't have to take a crosstown bus to get there. I just had to stroll down the alley to the back door. Whenever I arrived, the two cooks would stop their prep to turn and gawk as if I were walking down a runway rather than through their grubby kitchen. "Little girl! Little girl! Ooooh!" they said. I'd roll my eyes. Once, the grey-haired chef smacked the back of my denim skirt. I made sure he never did that again. I could have jabbed his eyes out with my pointing finger. "Don't you dare touch me again, *ever!*" I warned him.

Even though I was still dating Tyler, my attention was drifting toward a fellow employee at the restaurant, John, a gangling young man who worked as an accountant by day and drove delivery by night. I hadn't thought much of him at first, but the more I got to know him, the more I liked him. He had his own style, walked to his own swaggering beat and wasn't concerned with the fashions of the day, wearing a mullet, a stud earring and brightly coloured tank tops with either torn jeans or sweats he'd cut into shorts. He had a sense of humour, and his eyes twinkled when he laughed. And he would clear my tables when the restaurant was busy, then refuse a cut of my tips.

It wasn't long before I could no longer ignore the fact that I was developing strong feelings for him, feelings that I knew he had as well, so I was forced to think hard about my relationship with Tyler. We'd been arguing for months now. I can't remember what the arguments were about, but I was coming to realize that the relationship was never going to work. When we broke up, Granny said, "Lots of mothers would give their right arm for their daughter to date a boy like Tyler." I knew she was right. I'll never forget how good he was to my mother or how good his mother was to me. He was a great guy; he just wasn't the guy for me.

I soon discovered that John was quite the outdoorsman and spent most of his spare time exploring the backcountry. As we drove dusty gravel roads in his rusty Toyota four-by-four (his ticket to great fishing holes), I was reminded of my childhood days in the Cariboo. One afternoon in a secluded coastal bay, he showed me how to cast using a lure he'd fashioned himself, his body leaning into mine, his strong hands touching mine. What a thrill to catch a rockfish for dinner! He cleaned it right then and there, throwing the remains into the water, where we watched little crabs scurry over to claim them. Then he grilled our catch on his mini hibachi, serving a salad on the side with the fixings he'd brought. To complete the banquet, he cracked open a bottle of wine.

What I admired most about John was his confidence. Once, when we went crabbing off a public pier, an older fellow who looked like he could have modelled for *GQ* magazine in his younger days announced that our catch was undersized. But John, who had a huge respect for nature, was not a bit intimidated, and he turned to me and said, loud enough for all to hear, "Don't you hate back-seat drivers?"

──✱──

I was still making time for my mother, and one day at the beginning of July we met at the rose garden in Stanley Park. She looked pretty with her hair down, the style she preferred lately. After admiring the vibrant flowers, we made a game of finding which roses smelled best. How silly we were, giggling as we skittered from shrub to shrub, sniffing the various perfumes while sightseers mingled nearby. We decided that the yellow ones were the most aromatic, and we were still laughing when, as we walked back along the trail to catch the bus, she surprised me by saying that she'd stopped taking her medication.

"What do you mean, Mom? I don't think that's so good."

"I don't like the side effects," she said.

I couldn't understand why after all these years she had decided she didn't like the side effects, but I did understand that if any doctor, a psychiatrist or otherwise, prescribed medication, it was for a good reason and should be taken. I decided I should let her psychiatrist know.

When we got back to her apartment complex, as she was unlocking the door, the manager walked by, but he didn't say hello. Instead, he snickered and asked if any men had been talking outside her apartment lately. She ignored him, while I made no comment, thinking that there must have been a party and drunken men must have been loud in the halls. In fact, she had been hearing voices.

I was focused on getting her psychiatrist's number, and the opportunity occurred when she went to the bathroom. I retrieved her address book from the drawer, quickly flipped through its pages, found what I needed, wrote the number down on an old receipt, then closed the book and shut the drawer, all before Mom came out of the bathroom.

I didn't call right away, as she seemed all right. Maybe I was being paranoid, I told myself. Days later, when I called to wish Theo a happy birthday, I told Walter what Mom had said and asked if he thought I should make the call to her psychiatrist. I was taken aback when he answered sarcastically, as if I was wasting my time, "Yes, why don't you *do* that?"

Not understanding, I called anyway. Better to be safe. Over the coming days I spoke to an answering machine repeatedly, leaving my number and the same message every time, saying that I was Carolyn Anne's daughter, that my mother had gone off her medication and could she please call me? I don't know why, but I never heard from her. Maybe she was on vacation. Maybe she was overworked and didn't have the time. Maybe there were confidentiality policies I didn't know about. The result remains the same: while my mother was teetering on the edge of a faulty system, I was calling for help and nobody answered.

Some things have changed since then. Today it is possible to develop a "Ulysses Agreement" while a person is in recovery. This personalized care plan, initiated by the BC Schizophrenia Society, includes input from a support team outlining appropriate actions to take to help someone like my mother to feel safe and get better. Temporary care arrangements for minor children can also be included in the plan. Unfortunately, none of this was available when our little family needed it.

—∞—

One evening John dropped by to invite me to Sunday dinner at his sister's home in Port Coquitlam. I had already dined on my regular fare of a potato topped with cheese, but there was no way I'd turn down an invitation to spend time with my new catch. On the way there we drove past a series of institutional buildings on the north side of the road, and I had a sudden sense that I'd been there before.

"What is that place?"

"Oh, that's Riverview. It's a mental institution."

A hazy memory formed of going there with Granny when I was a tot, and I felt a rush of emotion when I realized my mother had been a patient there. But I didn't say anything to John. Within minutes, his family was welcoming me into their home: his precocious young nephews, his gentle-mannered sister and his boisterous brother-in-law. We enjoyed a fabulous roast beef dinner.

As we were heading back, John suggested we go back to his place to watch a movie and I agreed. But of all the hundreds of movies he had to choose, it was *One Flew Over the Cuckoo's Nest*. When I saw the jacket, I had immediate reservations but figured I'd try to make the best of it. However, after seeing a patient in restraints, the cold colourless rooms and the contemptuous Nurse Ratched, I couldn't take another moment of it.

"Turn it off, turn it off!" I cried, becoming an instant blubbering mess.

"Okay, okay!" John responded, confused but quickly pushing the off button on the remote.

My explanation came out as a series of nonsensical sentences, punctuated by sobbing gasps, as I left salty tears all over his shirt. "People! They're people!" I cried. "My mother! She's been in Riverview! She has schizophrenia!"

After I'd calmed down, I told him about the phone call, and he reassured me, "If you left a message with her psychiatrist, I'm sure she'll be okay."

Days later Ron and I went to see her. She told us she had slept with a man off the street, who had stolen her purse.

"What?" Ron and I said as she sat on her bed wearing a mischievous grin. "You can't sleep with just any guy off the street!" I didn't even want to picture it. We continued to talk about our mother as if she weren't there. Looking back, I realize she wasn't.

"She's trying to be like you, Phyllis," Ron said. "That's what she's doing. She knows you have a new boyfriend."

"But I don't sleep with just anyone off the street, Ron!" I countered.

While I thought her behaviour was unusual, part of me reasoned that perhaps Ron was right; perhaps she was having a mid-life crisis, just wanting to be young again. If she was looking for a good time and slept with a stranger who stole her wallet, surely that was her decision. I didn't think to ask if she needed help to replace her stolen money or ID. She was an adult, after all. She would manage.

Days later I was about to head out to Mom's because she wasn't answering her phone again when a friend called to invite me for a movie-night sleepover. "Your mom will be fine," she assured me. "I'll drive you over there first thing in the morning."

Ron had just come home from work, so I told him I'd be spending the night at my friend's place and left.

I didn't discover until the writing of these pages that about an hour after my departure, Mom had shown up at our apartment. Ron caught her searching through our things. "What are you doing?" he asked. She said she needed money. "Why don't you just ask instead of sneaking around?" he demanded. He figured he had embarrassed her, because she left hastily.

By that time I would have been watching a comedy at my friend's apartment. And while I was laughing, my mother was dying.

WAKE-UP CALL

If only I could turn back the clock,
If only I hadn't been in the dark,
If only I knew then what I know now,
Would it have mattered?
Too late

Sleeping,
Phone ringing,
Middle of the night.
Doom

Don't tell me the words I don't want to hear.
Don't tell me my mother is dead.
I don't want to believe she has left this world.
Darkness

Punch the walls,
Break them down,
Pillows don't soften the blows.
Futility

Ache in my heart,
Crumple to the floor,
A thousand tears,
Silence

Ten years later, after my grandmother had lost her final battle with cancer, my husband was killing time between work projects in the city when he came across an interview Granny and her husband had given to a newspaper reporter late in that fateful summer of 1990. Even though

I was thirty years old by the time he gave it to me, the information in the interview had been too difficult to deal with and I had just filed the article away. Now, as I was writing this book, I dug it out.

The parents of the woman shot and killed by police at a New Westminster SkyTrain station earlier this summer blame the provincial government for failing to provide adequate services for people with mental health problems.

In an exclusive interview with the *Record/Now*, Evelyn Smith said her daughter Carolyn Anne ... was the victim of a system that didn't provide her with the necessary services.

Smith, in a telephone interview from her home in Ottawa, said that "Carolyn was diagnosed as schizophrenic when she was 16 years old. From that time on she's struggled to cope with her illness and life."

Throughout her troubled life, Carolyn received little help from the government, Smith said. "While the system failed Carolyn I hope that it won't fail others. Carolyn was a victim of a system where her social needs and welfare were either inadequate or ignored."

In the end life must have become too hard for Carolyn, said Smith: "Things just started to pile up and she couldn't cope."

Smith said Carolyn received a monthly disability pension of $608 which was just enough to cover the bare necessities. "After spending about $400 on rent, $43 for her hydro and telephone bill, Carolyn was left with about $165 for groceries and other necessities."

Smith said she found very little food at her daughter's apartment when she visited after her daughter's death. "All I found in her fridge was some margarine, ketchup and a few sticks of celery."

Too few support services exist for people like Carolyn, she said.

"Early in January she was evicted from the building

she lived in because it was set to be demolished. Trying to find an affordable place to live put a lot of pressure on Carolyn. She was basically left on her own to find an apartment."

Smith said that led Carolyn to an overdose of pills and a short stay at a hospital. "What she needed was some medical supervision. Instead she was sent home to cope on her own."

C.A. Smith, Carolyn's stepfather, said some animals get better treatment than his stepdaughter.

"A lot of people don't recognize or respond to the needs of people with mental health problems."

While he didn't want to minimize the actions of his stepdaughter, Smith did question the necessity of shooting her twice. "The officer wasn't dealing with a big, husky and strapping girl. He was dealing with someone who was a little over five feet and weighed about 125 pounds. One bullet would have stopped Carolyn," he said.

"Carolyn did have a history of carrying a knife around with her to protect herself and she had a fear of men. But she had never harmed anyone before," he added.

Smith said he wonders why the officer didn't call for more help before the situation got out of hand. "But part of the problem may be that I just don't have enough information about the incident yet. We're still waiting to hear if there's going to be an inquest," he said.

Evelyn Smith said she hopes that what happened to Carolyn will help others. "I know that nothing we say will bring her back but I hope that her death will in some way arouse the feeling of those charged with the responsibility of administering to the 'Carolyn's' of this land. I can only hope that they will be moved to do what they can to make life better for the many sufferers of mental disorders." ...

Just six weeks before Carolyn's death her mother and stepfather came out west for a visit. "At that time there was no indication that things could go so wrong, so quickly," he said. ...[2]

While my grandmother hadn't told me about this passionate interview, she had told me about the inquest. She had asked if I wanted to go, but I hadn't wanted to hear my mother's death hashed over by strangers. My husband had also unearthed the coroner's report the same day he found the newspaper interview, though, as I had with the newspaper story, I had quickly filed it away. When I began writing this story, I dusted it off because it shows how, in less than a blind minute, my mother went from fighting with her hallucinations to fighting for her life. Even while she lay unconscious and bleeding, "other police officers assisted in handcuffing the woman." The coroner's report says:

> Carolyn Anne was a 45-year-old resident of New Westminster. ... She had been under the care of the New Westminster office of the Mental Health Association for the last 10 years and prior to that at the Burnaby office. Up until April 1990, she had been receiving medication every two weeks by injection at the Mental Health office. This medication was slow-acting and controlled her condition comfortably for the 2-week period.
>
> In April 1990 her medication was changed and on April 8, 1990, it was necessary for the New Westminster Police to assist ambulance personnel in restraining her. She had taken an overdose and was very violent and displayed suicidal tendencies. On this occasion she threatened the ambulance attendants with a knife. Since April 1990 she had only attended the Mental Health Clinic on two occasions.
>
> Reportedly, she had told her daughter in mid-July that she had not taken her medication for the past three months because of the side effects. Her psychiatrist ad-

---

2   Bessie Brown, "Cabinet Blamed for SkyTrain Shooting: Woman Shot by Cop Needed Better Care, Parents Say," *New Westminster Now*, September 9, 1990.

vised that non-compliance with the medication would result in a patient having the following symptoms—altered thinking processes, paranoia, delusions, distrustfulness, anxiety.

POSTMORTEM EXAMINATION: Toxicology analyses were performed on admission antemortem blood obtained prior to transfusion. Toxicology included analyses for ethyl alcohol, basic and acidic drug screens, opiates, cocaine and Trifluoperazine—all of which were completely negative for anti-psychotics suggesting that she had withdrawn from her medication.

Investigation was conducted by the New Westminster Police, Major Crime Section. A 38-caliber special snub-nosed revolver was given up for examination by investigation by [the officer involved in the shooting]. Follow-up investigation disclosed several important findings: On the New Westminster Police Department's Radio Room master tape, the sound of a female screaming was heard and documented at 2009 hours and 26 seconds. At 2009 hours and 27 seconds, two shots were fired within one second. The elapsed time from the officer's arrival at the scene until the shots were fired was 46 seconds.

[The officer] was examined and both elbows displayed noticeable fresh bruises. He provided blood samples which were negative for ethyl alcohol and drugs.

Death was attributed to massive hemorrhage due to gunshot laceration. Despite regaining consciousness and surgical intervention, there was irreversible shock leading to cardiac arrest.

CONCLUSION: I find that Carolyn Anne came to her death in New Westminster, BC, on July 24, 1990, from unnatural causes, to wit: gunshot wound to the abdomen.

I classify this death as "Homicide." Homicide is a death resulting from injuries caused directly or indirectly by the actions of another person without imputing blame or fault to that person.

I am of the opinion that the actions of [the officer] on July 24, 1990, were justified to protect himself and the general public.

—Coroner

MOTHER'S ASHES

I woke from another fitful night beside my husband, who was peacefully snoring. I looked at the clock. Five thirty. Too early to get up. I still had hours before meeting Ron in the city to spread Mom's ashes on what we saw as a fitting day: the twenty-fifth anniversary of her death. I hadn't been ready to part with them before now. Over the years I'd taken her ashes from my bedroom closet several times when the weight of her loss was especially heavy, and I had run my fingers through them as if I could feel her, touch her, wishing she were here. Then I would wipe away my tears, replace the box on the shelf and carry on with my life.

I had invited Walter to his sister's ash-spreading ceremony, feeling that I owed him that, but I wasn't completely surprised when he declined. Recently I'd told him over the phone that I wanted to look into the past, that I had questions about my mother's life, and he had brushed off my search for answers. "You should ask your aunt Lynn. She's older and probably knows more."

As I stared at the ceiling, I thought about my conversation with him when I finally asked the question I'd been saving far too long, saving for the right time that never seemed to come. So I just came right out with it. "Before you go, can you tell me if Uncle Jack has ever been to jail?"

"No, Phyllis. He's never been to jail."

"Oh, um … all right then … thanks. Goodbye." Click.

There it was: an answer that left me feeling off balance as I realized the only jail time Uncle Jack had ever served was in the dark recesses of my mind. I'd had suspicions about my childish notion starting from the time of the reunion, when it seemed surreal to be in the same room with him while everyone else was acting so normal. I became even more suspicious a few years later when I told Walter what Uncle Jack had done. "Don't you think your mom put that idea in your head?"

I wondered what Ron would say.

I glanced at the clock again. Nearly six. Might as well get up. I walked to the bathroom and looked in the mirror, asking myself if everyone else could see what I was: a troubled and exhausted soul. But no, I wasn't like some people who wear their lack of sleep in the bags under their eyes.

As my family slept, I dressed in the summer clothes I'd placed beside the container holding Mom's ashes, and my mind flashed back to the previous evening when, as I reached for it, my hand had fallen on the shoebox that contained my father's life. His sisters had sent it after he died, and it contained mainly the letters and pictures we'd exchanged in the decade or so he had been in my life. I had never imagined that my mother's ashes would bring my father to me.

Ron and I had never expected him to attend her funeral. It was not at all the meeting I'd imagined, with Mom's deathly shadow looming, draining any longing or excitement, but his sisters Sherry and Barbara had insisted it bothered them that he'd "never been there" for us, and they had generously paid his fare west. When I picked him up at the airport with a college friend escorting me, I'd masked my broken heart with a smile and a shy "Hi, Dad." I remember that he walked with a slight limp and looked much older than Mom, likely a result of his heavy drinking and smoking, and his speech was a slurred drawl. I also remember that we stopped at the liquor store and that, back at the apartment, he laughed when he told Ron and me about the night our mother had passed out after a couple of beers, trying to keep up with his drinking pace. "Yep, she was out cold."

Our mother may not have had enough support in life, but the provincial government provided for her in death, and we attended her welfare service in a funeral home across town. The pews were sparsely populated with family and a few of my supportive friends, and the air was filled with the preacher's drone, my grandmother's muffled sniffles and Ron's moaning cry on my shoulder. My own river of tears had dried up by then.

Years later, unable to attend my father's service, I had sent a heartfelt letter instead. Now, as I looked through the mementoes in the shoebox, even though I'd had them for years, I realized my letter wasn't there. I'd written something about how thankful I was for the time we had playing pool at his favourite pub the odd time I'd flown east to visit

Granny and that I appreciated our phone calls with messages of love—even if his words had been mixed with alcohol. "I love you too, Dad."

My aunt Barbara, who had delivered my message to him while he took his last breaths, told me I was "a classy lady." Not for long, though. She and my aunt Sherry insisted that Ron and I pay for his funeral with the meagre insurance money he had left us, and I quickly went from "a classy lady" to "trash." I had explained that we wanted to follow our father's dying wishes that we keep the money, but my aunts would have nothing of it. It wasn't until John grabbed the phone that they understood. "Where have you been all their lives? What have you ever done for them?" I haven't heard a peep from them since. No more Christmas cards. No more baby gifts. Only a shoebox filled with heartache.

After a light breakfast I woke John with a soft kiss. "Have a good day," he said. He had plans to work from home and then take the girls fishing, as they love being on the water as much as he does. If they caught a keeper, he said, he would grill salmon for dinner.

I tiptoed to wake Anne next, the daughter who bears my mother's middle name. I softly whispered her name and her eyes flew open. It has always been amazing to me that she can sleep through practically anything but always wakes to my whispers. She gave me a big hug. I knew she was worried for me.

"I'll be okay, honey. Have fun today."

Clutching my mother's ashes, I walked downstairs, where I could hear the deep, regular breathing of my older daughter, Eve, coming from her open doorway. I had bid her goodbye last night. She was a teen now and valued her sleep. I had worried for a time that I would forget the sound of my mother's laughter, but she reminds me every day.

⟶

Buzz! Buzz! "I'm here!" I called out.

"Coming!" Ron answered.

While driving through the light early-morning traffic to the cemetery, I told him what Walter had said, but it turned out that even he had known the answer I didn't. "You thought he was in jail? I think Uncle Jack *worked* at Oakalla as a security guard for a while, Phyllis, but he was never *in* jail. And he moved back to Ottawa when Granny moved back there." After realizing that this made sense of his absence,

I explained what Mom had said all those years ago when I was a child swinging back and forth on the swings at Deer Lake, as if between two worlds—the harsh world of judgment and the real world of emotions. "Prison is where bad people go." Like me, Ron figured I had put my uncle behind bars as a means of coping with the unthinkable.

Minutes later we stood on the path to the memorial rose garden, our mother's final resting place. Magnificent red maples stood watch nearby, their arms reaching to the sky like beacons of hope. I took comfort in knowing that our mother would rest in the same neighbourhood where our family of three had shared our lives, where we'd held hands as we walked to school, where we'd done our meagre grocery shopping and where we'd hung out at the nearby lake.

As we solemnly knelt in the sunshine among the fragrant blossoms, mixing our mother's dust with the soil, my thoughts took me back to that long-ago afternoon in Stanley Park when we had smelled the roses together. And I felt a sense of peace knowing that my mother's cinders would nourish beautiful blossoms, the same kind of blossoms that had once brought her joy. We ended our little ceremony with teary eyes, a warm embrace and a silent promise. We will always love you.

LAST WORDS

It was the summer of 2016, the late afternoon sun as piercing as Walter's eyes when he spoke his last words to me. My family had spent a few hours at a public park, and, leaving them to explore, I walked to Walter and Stacy's cottage a short distance away. I wanted to ask why they hadn't returned my calls since they had wrapped up our family day at the beach with a hot dog roast the previous summer. As I entered the yard, Stacy, her hair now lined with grey, was in a recliner soaking up sunshine and wine. Though startled to see me, she greeted me politely and then went inside to tell Walter I was there. I wasn't invited in. "We'll meet you at the park in a few minutes," she said when she returned.

I agreed reluctantly, then walked back down the trail and perched on a log bench from where I could still hear the soft chatter of John and the girls. When my aunt and uncle showed up, they settled themselves into folding deck chairs, my uncle, with his thinning hair, looking more like his late father than ever. While we made small talk, Stacy was cheerful, possibly from drink, but Walter was aloof and wouldn't look at me. When I eventually asked why I hadn't heard from them, he kept his eyes to the ground. He didn't want to talk about it, he said.

Frustrated, I asked, "Can't you at least tell me what's going on?"

That's when he turned to me with the same look in his eyes as that long-ago day when I was seventeen and moved out of his house. "You're too much work," he said.

In the days that followed, through bouts of tears, I cried, "But they're family!"

"They're just your aunt and uncle, Phyllis!" John countered. "Lots of people don't keep in touch with their aunts and uncles. I haven't even met some of mine in Europe. Don't you see? We're your family now, me and our daughters!"

I found myself recalling the day Stacy had proudly shared with me the album of all the pictures she'd taken of the boys' high school graduations, though she hadn't bothered to attend mine. And I remembered a potluck party before the boys had grown and scattered in different directions. "I can't wait to be a grandfather!" Walter had said, turning to Ron and me. "When are you going to have kids so we can spoil them and send them home?" And he had turned to Stacy, who had smiled complacently.

They hadn't "spoiled" my school-aged daughters, in Walter's sense of the word, when they agreed to take care of them one weekend a few years earlier while John and I attended a wedding. While Walter and Stacy reported they'd had a good time playing cards with the girls, Eve disagreed. "We had to clean the house!" she complained.

I laughed and said, "Welcome to my childhood! A few chores never hurt anybody."

"It's not funny, Mom!" Eve said. "It's one thing to ask us to tidy our own mess, but it's another to ask us to tidy *their* mess when we only just got there! I had to hang Walter's underwear on the clothesline!"

And at last I began to understand that, because of my lack of family, I had been desperate for family. Any family, I thought, was better than no family. It must have been the same for Ron, but his relationship with Walter and Stacy had petered out much earlier. "Whenever I tried to meet with them," he told me, "they were always busy." Like my brother, I was at last tired of trying. Perhaps the reality was that they didn't need us anymore.

The boys grew up long ago, but we've stayed in touch. When they occasionally mention their parents, I feel a twinge of longing, but, like some friends who come and go, my aunt and uncle have come and gone. I have my own family.

⸺⸺

A few months ago, on an unusually warm winter day, my brother and I went back to the neighbourhoods where we had resided with our mother. I had found the addresses on some life insurance papers in a plastic folder of Mom's that I hadn't bothered to open until then. As we approached Royal Oak Avenue in Burnaby, my eyes lit up in recognition when I saw the recreation centre. "That's where we took swimming lessons!"

"Yeah, I remember!" Ron said. "I hated going into the girl's change room!" We laughed.

The building hadn't aged as we had. If anything, the place looked younger, altered to fit into what had become a more upscale community than the neighbourhood of our past. Moments later and a few blocks away, as I pulled up at the curb, I commented, "This is the place where our house used to be." But there was no house there now, just grass. "Makes me think that after it burned down, it was never rebuilt."

"Yeah, looks that way," Ron agreed. "So that means that this house"—he pointed to the stucco house on the corner—"would have been Betty's."

It looked smaller than I remembered, but I said, "Yep, it must be."

"I remember hanging out among all the industrial buildings," he said.

"And I remember running down the railway tracks," I said. Gazing down those tracks set on their crumbly, dry gravel bed was like looking into a past that would become my future and eventually fade away with time into the past again.

"It's amazing that little corner store is still here," Ron said, glancing across the street.

We drove down our walking route to school. Like Betty's house, the school was smaller than I remember, but the walk was longer. It was hard to believe how far our little legs had carried us, how strong we had been.

We searched for our Norfolk Street home next and were surprised to discover that no house stood at that address either. Unlike the upscale community we'd just left, this community had become aged and rundown. A shiny new house or two stood out among the others, but most looked sad. "But there's the alley where I learned to ride my bike!" I said.

As I drove to our next destination, a city park, I couldn't help but think how odd it was that no homes exist today in the places where our unassuming family of three had dreamed of happier days. But as we walked one of the nature trails, Ron turned to me and said, "Our mother hasn't left us, you know. Her spirit lives in the deep blue sky. Her spirit lives in the blooming plants. Her spirit lives in our hearts." Then we hugged and continued our newly rekindled family tradition of enjoying the sunshine at Deer Lake, just the three of us, like old times.

A year later I returned home after keeping up the tradition to find my daughters sipping sodas at the kitchen bar and chattering to John while he prepared a seafood dinner. When they asked me about my day, with lightness in my voice and glistening tears in my eyes, I was able to tell my daughters for the first time about the long-ago days when their uncle Ron and I had bathed in sunshine and splashed in laughter with the mother we loved and still love as if there were no heaviness in the world.

As time passed I talked about my mother more and more, and one day I even baked a macaroni casserole for my family. When I saw the strings of cheese hanging off their forks, I announced, "My mother used to make this. It was my favourite!" Another day, when Eve added a ton of crackers to her bowl of mushroom soup, I told her, "You're just like your grandmother. She always ate her soup with lots of crackers!"

While on a walk one brilliant evening, I paused to take in the horizon. Wishing my mother could stand with me to admire the beautiful view of the coastal mountains and the glittering Pacific, I raised my gaze to a flock of seagulls drifting on thermal uptakes in a looping pattern. One of these winged gliders broke away to soar off majestically in its own direction.

I turned toward home, knowing that my mother's love has always been with me and would stand by me the rest of my days.

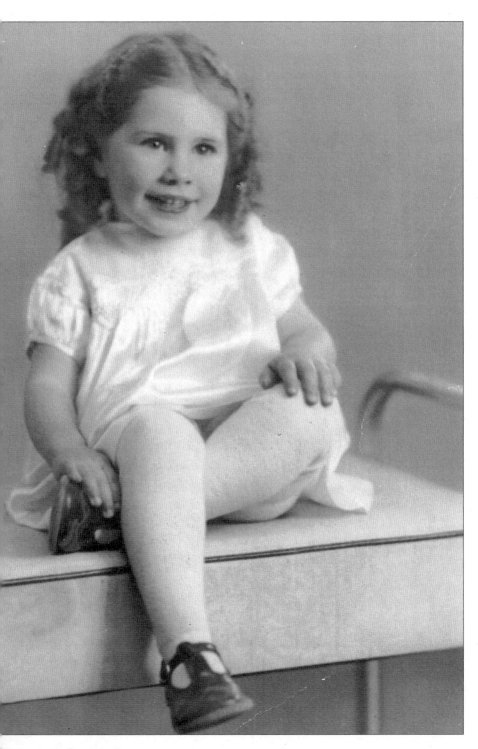

My mother, Carolyn.

ACKNOWLEDGEMENTS

I couldn't have written this book without the support of many. I'd like to thank Ursula, my long-time friend, soul sister and encouraging first reader; Melissa, for her unrelenting support and friendship; Sara and Laurie, for all the walks early on as I processed information; and Dave, for cheering me on. I'd also like to thank Lisa, Sharon and Curtis for their years of support and friendship. I believe this story wouldn't have been published without Ian and his friend Lauren, whose feedback on my first draft helped me to see what I couldn't. Thank you, Ian, for opening the door to Caitlin Press, and thank you, Sarah Corsie and Vici Johnstone, for inviting me in. I am ever thankful to the talented Betty Keller for making my story stronger, to Meg Yamamoto for her attention to detail and to Malaika Aleba for helping make my story visible.

I appreciate local branch members of the BC Schizophrenia Society, particularly Julie, Donna, Martha and Marilyn for embracing me into a circle of acceptance and for teaching me along the way, Lisa P. for providing information on Ulysses Agreements and Carol for helping me understand mental health disorders more deeply. Thank you to the late David Hume for believing that I would do something big one day because I care. This is it! I'd also like to thank Donna S. I will always cherish our days of "Reaching Out" to local high schools.

Many colleagues have inspired me: the other Ursula in my life for leading with fearless passion, Vanessa for leading mental health initiatives and Kirsten for technological support in my early days of promoting mental health awareness. Thank you, Terry, for working alongside me and sharing life experiences. I'd also like to acknowledge Debbie, Michelle and Robin for their unconditional listening and Kate for her regular check-ins.

I am grateful to the Dyson clan for welcoming me with open arms. A special thank you to my mother's sister and dear aunt for photos and filling in many gaps. Thank you to my unofficial sister-in-law for insight regarding government documents. I need to wrap my arms around my brother, who shared many of these experiences and talked about situations I knew were difficult. Big hugs to my children for their flexibility so I could write. A and E, I am so proud to be your mother. You teach me every day. My story is for you and your generation.

There are no words to express my appreciation for my kind-hearted flute teacher, whose presence has shaped me immensely and whose gift of music will ever remain a positive force in my life.

I wouldn't have made it here without my husband. Thank you for reminding me about balance and for holding me together when I felt I would crumble.

ABOUT THE AUTHOR

Phyllis Dyson is an elementary school teacher who holds a bachelor of arts in music and a graduate diploma in special education. A member of the BC Schizophrenia Society, she has promoted mental health awareness in her community through a program called Partnership. She lives in a small town on BC's West Coast with her husband and two daughters, where she enjoys hiking, playing her flute and boating with her family. She is proud to say that *Among Silent Echoes* is her first book.